Lead On!

Motivational Lessons for School Leaders

Pete Hall

Eye On Education
6 Depot Way West, Suite 106
Larchmont, NY 10538
(914) 833-0551
(914) 833-0761 fax
www.eyeoneducation.com

Library of Congress Cataloging-in-Publication Data

Hall, Peter A., 1971–
Lead on! : motivational lessons for school leaders/Pete Hall.
      p.   cm.
Includes bibliographical references.
ISBN 978-1-59667-201-7
1. School management and organization.
2. Educational leadership. 3. Motivation in education.
I. Title.
LB2805.H255 2011
371.2—dc23   2011037093

10 9 8 7 6 5 4 3 2 1

Sponsoring Editor: Robert Sickles
Production Editor: Lauren Beebe
Copyeditor: Kahini Ranade
Designer and Compositor: Matthew Williams, click! Publishing Services
Cover Designer: Dave Strauss, 3FoldDesign

Also Available from EYE ON EDUCATION

The Principal's Guide to the First 100 Days of the School Year:
Creating Instructional Momentum
Shawn Joseph

What Great Principals Do *Differently*:
18 Things That Matter Most (2nd Edition)
Todd Whitaker

The Fearless School Leader:
Making the Right Decisions
Cynthia McCabe

Communicate and Motivate:
The School Leader's Guide to Effective Communication
Shelly Arneson

Principals Who Dare to Care
A. William Place

Improving Your Daily Practice:
A Guide for Effective School Leadership
Timothy B. Berkey

The 4 CORE Factors for School Success
Todd Whitaker & Jeffrey Zoul

Motivating and Inspiring Teachers:
The Educational Leader's Guide for
Building Staff Morale (2nd Edition)
Todd Whitaker, Beth Whitaker, & Dale Lumpa

Leading School Change:
9 Strategies to Bring Everybody On Board
Todd Whitaker

The Principalship from A to Z
Ronald Williamson & Barbara R. Blackburn

About the Author

Pete Hall is currently the principal of Shaw Middle School, a Title I school in Spokane, Washington. After a teaching career that spanned three states and included primary, intermediate, and middle-school positions, Mr. Hall served as principal of Anderson Elementary School in Reno, Nevada. When he took over Anderson Elementary in 2002, it was the only school in Nevada to have failed to make AYP for four consecutive years. Two short years later, it was the only Title I school in the state of Nevada to earn "High Achieving" designation. Subsequently, Mr. Hall served as the principal of Sheridan Elementary, a Title I school in Spokane, which earned accolades from the Washington State Office of the Superintendent for its growth and achievement. His leadership works include authoring over a dozen articles on leadership and publishing two books, *The First-Year Principal* (Scarecrow Education, 2004) and *Building Teachers' Capacity for Success: A collaborative guide for coaches and school leaders* (ASCD, 2008). He is also a popular columnist of Education World (www.educationworld.com).

For his tenacious and courageous leadership, Mr. Hall has been honored with ASCD's Outstanding Young Educator Award (2004), Nevada's Martin Luther King Jr Award (2005), and Phi Delta Kappa's Emerging Leaders Award (2009), among others. He was appointed to the Governor's Commission on Excellence in Education (in Nevada, 2005) and was selected to sit on the National Education Association's Great Public Schools Indicators Advisory Panel (2010–2011). He holds a National Principal Mentor Certificate from NAESP and serves as a trainer and coach for NAESP's PALS mentoring program. He has worked as a personal consultant/motivational coach for professional athletes, weekend golfers, stand-up comedians, firefighters, business executives, custodians, and more. He speaks and consults internationally. Get more information at www.educationhall.com, contact him via e-mail at petehall@educationhall.com, follow him on Twitter at @EducationHall, or call his cell at (208) 755-3139.

Acknowledgments

I owe giant debts of gratitude to all the individuals, educators or otherwise, who have supported, encouraged, inspired, and simultaneously endured me throughout my development as a leader, as an author, and as a person. To attempt to acknowledge you all by name, in this space, would be fruitless and would consume reams of paper. To streamline matters, I'll confine this list to those whose contributions are directly reflected in this book project.

First honors go to the good people at www.EducationWorld .com, in particular Vice President Rich Datz, whose support and flexibility have been essential to the creation of this true partnership, and former Editor-in-Chief Gary Hopkins, whose persistence and brainstorming prowess have resulted in a collaborative project of which we're all quite proud. Likewise, I thank the staff at Eye On Education, namely CEO Bob Sickles, who bizarrely is both a Yankees fan *and* good at heart. We were able to get past our baseball conflicts and focus on this project for the benefit of children and educators everywhere. Also, big, big thanks to Production Editor Lauren Beebe, who has been an absolute joy to work with—I don't presume to believe she'd say the same, since I can be rather stubborn about the inclusion of my many off-color remarks and incoherent babble.

To my parents Cliff and Alice, whose words and deeds led me to be the person I am today, I offer this: you've quite wittingly created an irreverent, conscientious educator. Congratulations and thank you! To my lovely and talented wife Mindy, who coincidentally is the best teacher I've ever seen work, thank you for putting up with my long, late hours at the computer after long, late hours at work. And to my children: Daniel, Indy, and Peja, and the millions of kids like them across the globe, I dedicate this book with the expectation that anyone who reads it is as interested in making top-flight education a reality as I am. You deserve outstanding, dedicated, motivated teachers and principals. Here's to you.

—Pete Hall, Coeur d'Alene, ID, October 2011

Contents

Introduction

I never planned to be a teacher, let alone one bent on changing the face of education. As a child, I was fully preparing to become the shortstop for the Boston Red Sox; that goal sat in my pocket well beyond its expiration date as I continued to grow up and grow further away from that dream. I could imagine myself smoothing the dirt between second and third base at Fenway Park in Boston awaiting a ground ball I could gobble up and fire to first to the delight of 35,000 fans. But I never envisioned myself in the front of a classroom without anyone cheering or starting The Wave around the room, delivering lessons that would inspire children and would prepare them for a life of success and opportunity.

I had been a pretty good athlete as a youngster, and fortunately my boyhood basketball coach, Nelson Mills, saw enough potential in me that he invited me to serve as an assistant coach for the youth teams he continued to lead in Corvallis, Oregon. It was through that very short, eye-opening experience that I realized what an effect one individual can have upon another.

Even as an assistant youth-league basketball coach who was barely older than the players I was coaching, I could guide the kids—mold them, inspire them, challenge them, and extend their own self-imposed limits. The impact, it turned out, rarely had much to do with basketball, either. These were lives we were talking about, futures we were nurturing, fellow humans we were helping to develop. Sure, some of those eighth-graders were already taller than I was, and the possibilities before them were endless, the opportunities profound. I had found my niche. I was destined to become a teacher.

The teaching path took me through terrific towns: West Sacramento, California; Boston, Massachusetts (surprised?); Livermore, California; and Reno, Nevada.

My Personal Leadership Mentors

School leadership first piqued my interest while I was in Reno, Nevada the "Biggest Little City in the World." As a classroom teacher, I paid strict attention to the principals leading my buildings. Each had a lesson to teach me, either through their words or deeds, that sticks with me still.

From Dave Lannigan, I learned to keep myself healthy as a person. He emphasized that stress is created within ourselves; when we're happy, well-adjusted, balanced people, we'll be better educators. He practiced what he preached, taking steps to keep himself on an even keel.

Dave was often on the golf course by 4:30 on school days, much to the chagrin of many teachers and parents seeking advice or a meeting with the principal. However, he was resolute, leaving the toils and troubles of the schoolhouse behind, trading them instead for the bunkers and whiffs he so often laughed about on the links. He never took himself, or anything around him, too seriously. This allowed him to recharge his batteries, so he always came in refreshed the next day.

From Debbie Cylke, I learned about motivation. Debbie was, and still is, a phenomenal speaker. She challenged her staff to continuously move toward improvement, whether it was instructionally or relationally. One of her favorite sayings was, "Attitude determines altitude," and she demanded excellence at every turn.

One day, Debbie came to our team meeting requesting a volunteer to tackle some additional responsibilities around campus. I don't remember what the details were, but I'm sure they weren't glamorous. All I recall is this: Before she was finished asking for help, I was (metaphorically) on my knees begging her to select me for the role. She had a knack for motivating those around her to take action and to extend ourselves.

From Frank Garrity, I learned to be tough. Frank and I had simultaneously arrived as principal and assistant principal, respectively, at an elementary school that was in dire need of a makeover. Labeled "persistently dangerous" and underachieving academically, our elementary school demanded presence, grit, commitment, and more than a fair share of motivational techniques for the troops in the trenches.

Frank, a former fighter-jet pilot instructor and reincarnation of John Wayne, led the way. He showed me how to confront mediocrity and incompetence, how to relish the confrontations between people as opportunities to grow and make effective changes, and how embracing the dirty work eventually leads to tremendous gains and brighter days.

And Into the Office We Go

Absorbing all the leadership lessons I could along the way, I felt like I was prepared to take on my first principalship when the opportunity presented itself. In 2002, our superintendent offered me the reins at Anderson Elementary School in Reno, Nevada. Anderson School was a Title I elementary school that had a 90 percent poverty rate and where 60 percent of the students were English-language learners; it was the only school in the state of Nevada to have failed to make its Adequate Yearly Progress (AYP) goals for four consecutive years. The outgoing principal had hand-selected eight teachers to join her at a new school that opened south of town, leaving many openings to fill. We were facing sanctions related to the No Child Left Behind Act, and the pressure was on. I'd have to rely on the lessons I'd learned from my mentors to make this work.

Being thrown headlong into the fire was perhaps the most wonderful experience I've ever enjoyed in education—how else could I measure exactly what I'm made of? How else could I shatter the limits of low expectations, inspire those around me to strive for continuous improvement, and usher an entire community into an era of confidence, pride, and renewed vigor?

Here's the short version of what happened next:

In my first year, we bonded as a team and agreed upon a comprehensive schoolwide improvement plan. We sorted through all the details, signed our commitments, measured our vital signs, and prepared for battle.

In year two, we implemented the plan: built-in collaboration, increased focus on literacy skills, goal-setting, smart use of formative assessments, professional development, and a ridiculously high level of energy. When the test scores came back, we expected to see growth. What we received, à la *Stand and Deliver*, was borderline miraculous. What was once the bane of Nevada's school system was indeed the State's only Title I school to garner "High Achieving" designation for its success in moving students to proficient or higher on state assessments.

In our third year, we built upon our strengths, continued to show growth, added on-site instructional coaching, and handled the barrage of school teams visiting our campus to observe, scrutinize, and copy some of the structures and elements we'd put in place to realize our success.

In year four, our community partnerships ran so strong and so deep that we held a 50th anniversary celebration gala for the school's Literacy Fund. We raised a whopping and poetic $50,050 to help struggling students learn to read. This was a school on the move.

Lessons Learned and Lessons Shared

The successes of Anderson Elementary School were dramatic, yes, but not surprising. The way I saw it, the latent potential in a school full of 500 students is not unlike a reservoir sitting behind a dam. It simply needed a valve, a crack, or a change agent to set the terrific power free.

Around the time that Anderson was receiving national attention for its rapid ascent, the good folks at EducationWorld .com contacted me, asking if I'd like to share my thoughts on leadership with my fellow principals online. Reluctant to consider myself a bona fide expert but thrilled to have the opportunity to share some strategies and approaches that worked, I acquiesced. Thus, the idea of these essays was born. Originally, my charge was to bring real-world advice to life, sharing practical tips that principals could implement immediately. As the contributions mounted, I found it exceedingly difficult to separate "advice" from "motivation," and, not seeing a need to keep them in separate corners anyway, I have married the two around the big idea of motivational leadership.

Two big lessons have emerged from my work as a school principal that I wanted somehow to convey. The first, driven by the accelerated pace of change needed at Anderson School, was about ownership. I might have conjured up the best ideas in the world, the plans that would place the school on the mountaintop, and the brilliant innovations that would result in 100 percent proficiency in everything. But if I couldn't get the buy-in from the staff, they would've just been mad ideas from the raving lunatic principal. Without the unilateral support of my personnel, I'd have been pressing the gas pedal to the floor while the gearbox stayed in neutral; we wouldn't have gone anywhere.

When I began at the spectacularly underachieving Anderson School, I was told that certain change initiatives would fail, that, "We've tried things like that before," and "Good luck pushing the boulder up that hill." I never believed our efforts would result in anything less than extraordinary gains; on the contrary, I viewed success as the only viable option. The key was to take the critical elements of effective schools and recreate them at Anderson—with the staff owning the changes, the innovations, and the structures. It was tedious, terrifying work—often we stood at the precipice of a potentially terrible direction—but with concerted efforts and intentional discussions with key stakeholders, we were able to steer things in the right direction. The plan, as you've read, was a tremendous success.

This experience taught me about the importance of garnering universal backing: motivating the masses to tackle the challenges together. As the leader, I can't make everything happen all by myself, but I can influence others to carry out our well-crafted plans. Where others fail is in lacking the belief that their efforts will yield benefits—a shortage of effort optimism. A dearth of confidence. A deficit of influence. It's this theory that is captured in Kerry Patterson and his colleagues' 2008 book, *Influencer: The Power to Change Anything*:

> The reason most of us pray for serenity rather than doggedly seeking a new solution to what ails us is that, left to our own devices, we don't come up with the big ideas

that solve the problems that have us stumped. We fall into the serenity trap every time we seek solace when we should be seeking a solution. To bring this problem to its knees, we first have to see ourselves as influencers. This revised self-image calls for a deviation from the existing norm. Rarely do people say that they currently are, or that one day they will be, an influencer . . .

We typically don't think of ourselves as influencers because we fail to see that the common thread running through most of the triumphs and tragedies of our lives is our ability to exert influence. If we did, we'd invest enormous energy in looking for new and better ways to enhance our influence repertoire. (p. 7)

The second lesson is one that has been confirmed over the years since I departed Anderson School, first at Sheridan Elementary and now at Shaw Middle School, both in Spokane, Washington. If this statement seems plain and straightforward, that's because it is: Every situation is unique. What works in one location, with one staff, in one school, in one community won't always work somewhere else where the variables are different. I've read articles about turnaround schools across the nation. My teaching staffs have engaged in book studies on "what works" and "best practices" in instructional approaches. There is no shortage of leadership texts clogging the shelves of most leaders' offices, mine included.

Effective leaders consider all the variables before creating a plan. They examine the culture. They evaluate the personnel. They scrutinize the history. They investigate the data. They research the stakeholders. They appraise the conditions of change. They sift through stacks of policies and protocol from the district office. They explore their expectations. In short, they weigh all of their options.

Why is this important? We know that leaders have immeasurable impact on organizations, so much so, in fact, that a school with an effective principal would outperform one with an ineffective principal seven days a week, all other factors remaining equal. A leader with a preordained agenda, then, would be counterproductive to the success of the school. The leader must take all the other variables into consideration prior to taking any action. Jim Collins (2001) explains this idea in his seminal leadership work, *Good to Great*, which sits dog-eared, highlighted, and practically mutilated on my own shelf of leadership resources. Mr. Collins describes a characteristic of the most effective leaders, those which he deems "Level 5 leaders":

> Level 5 leaders channel their ego needs away from themselves and into the larger goal of building a great company. It's not that Level 5 leaders have no ego or self-interest. Indeed, they are incredibly ambitious—but their ambition is first and foremost for the institution, not themselves. (p. 21)

How Can You Use This Book?

Lead On! was inspired by several essays on EducationWorld .com, which have been updated and incorporated into this book. The essays are organized into four categories: pure motivation, embracing change, surviving the day, and the principalship. This book is for anyone with a hand in (or an eye on) school leadership. Principals, assistant principals, superintendents, district office personnel, teacher leaders, department chairs, mentors, and anyone on a leadership team or in a leadership position will all find nuggets and bullion to cherish and share. The book addresses universal leadership themes, crossing elementary-middle-high school borders and even extending into the preschool and university ranks. The essays are a blend of my attempts at humor, some esoteric facts, some specific actions around multiple leadership topics, and a motivational theme that serves as the glue that holds everything together.

Each essay can stand alone as a piece of the professional growth puzzle. Each can be used as an excerpt to share with teachers, administrators, or leadership teams to launch an initiative or to build a common language. Or they can be used en masse as a way for us to calibrate our leadership settings on the most important elements of our work. These are meant to be timeless, kept at the bedside or on the office desk for easy, repeated reference, and shared with new leaders, colleagues, or those considering leadership roles in education.

Here are a few examples of how these essays have been used by educational leaders across the country, and some suggestions on how they could be implemented most effectively:

A superintendent wants her principals to engage in more frequent, consistent, meaningful walkthroughs. She brings the principals together, they read "Get Out of That Chair," and that launches their discussion on why, how, and when they'll tackle walkthroughs together.

A principal gathers the site leadership team together to revise the School Improvement Plan. At the beginning of the year, he copies and distributes "Hope Ain't a Strategy" to help the team embrace the idea of considering specific action steps. Then, toward the middle of October, he copies and distributes "Less Is More" to open the conversation about what they will take off the plate for each new initiative they add.

Around the anticipated beginning of spring after a long, dreary winter, when everyone is exhausted, stressed out, and ready to apply for other jobs, the department chair pulls out "Making It Fun Again" and shares it with her team. They follow by compiling a list of all the things that are going well, create a plan to recognize and celebrate what's right in their world, revitalize their commitment to education, and proceed to kick tail on the state exams the following month!

It's up to you. The words that follow are only as motivational as you allow them to be. However, greatness is within your reach, so reach already!

PART I

Get Motivated

The idea of motivation is not new. Since the dawn of time, no, even before that; way back at the crack of midnight the night before time dawned, we've sought ways to increase our motivation. How do we inspire groups of people to take action? What strategies can we use to encourage individuals to work harder, better, and faster? What can we rely upon to push and advance *ourselves* to strive? These questions and more have often sat at the heart of the matter for organizational leaders in the business world, in education, and in social assemblies.

But good heavens, where do we start? I searched for "motivation" online and returned over 30 million hits in a fraction of a second. That is a lot of articles, theories, ideas, theses, videos, speeches, strategies, suggestions, and approaches! In times like these, I turn to a couple of trusted resources: Marcus Buckingham and Daniel Pink.

Mr. Buckingham, a former researcher with the Gallup Organization, is the author of several leadership texts from the private sector. He has also authored books that I have used in my schools and seminars to lead in-depth discussions about strengths, management styles, and increased efficiency in organizations. In fact, I've read, reread, quoted, and paraphrased Mr. Buckingham's work so often I sometimes feel he's in the room helping guide the discussions. In his influential work, *The One Thing You Need to Know . . . About Great Managing, Great Leading, and Sustained Individual Success*, Mr. Buckingham implores those of us in leadership roles to tackle the strategy that fits our needs:

To excel as a manager you must never forget that each of your direct reports is unique and that your chief responsibility is not to eradicate this uniqueness, but rather to arrange roles, responsibilities, and expectations so that you can capitalize upon it.

To excel as a leader requires the opposite skill. You must become adept at calling upon those needs we all share. Our common needs include the need for security, for community, for authority, and for respect, but for you, the leader, the most powerful universal need is our need for clarity.

And last, you must remember that your sustained success depends on your ability to cut out of your working life those activities, or people, that pull you off your strengths' path. . . . It will always be your responsibility to make the small but significant course corrections that allow you to sustain your highest and best contribution to the team, and to the better future it is charged with creating. (p. 284)

Mr. Pink, meanwhile, speaks exclusively of motivation in his 2009 book, *Drive: The Surprising Truth about What Motivates Us*. In an argument describing a new era of workers and working environments, Mr. Pink posits that carrots and sticks are no longer the answer for mobilizing people toward greater productivity and a healthier output. The times of rewards and punishments have come and gone. Doing this actually makes them lose motivation in the long run. Rather, he claims, it's our responsibility to tap into people's intrinsic motivation. He categorizes as Type I behavior an extensive concern with the inherent satisfaction of the activity rather than of the rewards the activity brought. He described it thus:

Ultimately, Type I behavior depends on three nutrients: autonomy, mastery, and purpose. Type I behavior is self-directed. It is devoted to becoming better and better at something that matters. And it connects that quest for excellence to a larger purpose.

Some might dismiss notions like these as gooey and idealistic, but the science says otherwise. The science confirms that this sort of behavior is essential to being human—and that now, in a rapidly changing economy, it is also critical for professional, personal, and organizational success of any kind. (pp. 80–81)

Both offer insights into the world of motivation, and both contributions give us a glimpse into why motivation is such a complicated, beguiling, and tantalizing proposition: It's rarely the same for any two groups, teams, organizations, or people. It changes over time, alters with the circumstances, and moves like the wind.

The key, then, is to be on top of our games. If we're truly going to inspire, to encourage, to coax, to initiate, to stimulate, to light, to move, and to empower others (and *ourselves*), we must prepare a game plan. The first section of this book, which includes ten essays on the art of motivation of one sort or another, is an attempt to provide you some foundational tools. Whether you're launching an initiative, beginning a school year, gathering a committee, or just looking for a little pick-me-up (or "a kick in the arse," as my friend Mickey would say), Part I has got you covered.

Some of the essays, such as my bedrock "Always Strive to Be a Better You" and "Hope Ain't a Strategy," have decidedly philosophical bents. Others, including "The True Beauty of Goals," get a little more practical. Each is intended to make us, the readers, think more deeply about the activities we engage in as leaders, workers, and individuals; more importantly, we reflect upon *how* we pursue those activities. Some will resonate with you more than others. You might find a golden ticket among the wrappers, a little piece of encouragement for those down days that you'll flag and share with colleagues when the going gets rough. By no means have I provided to anyone The Answer; instead, all that I expect is that I've offered some motivation for you to ask and attack The Question with a bit more ferocity and vigor. Let's get motivated.

Always Strive to Be a Better You

In the 1950s and 1960s, novelist Ian Fleming created a character for a series of books, a secret agent whose triple-digit identity is as well known today as any string of numbers worldwide. He also gave his spy a mantra: "Live and let die." For 007, James Bond, whose professional and private lives intertwined quite intimately, that four-word phrase gave definition and direction to his very existence.

I believe in the power of a motto. When it's utilized deeper than just as a tagline, a motto can offer a very clear, literally spelled-out reminder of what drives us as individuals. It can be a printed inner voice, conjuring images of the ideal. Like an alarm clock or the howling horn of the 6:00 eastbound express, a mantra contains the power to jolt us headlong toward our goals.

Many years ago, I adopted this credo: "Always strive to be a better you." Its origins sprout from the ancient Greek philosophy of paideia, which espouses the belief that life's true goal is to attain one's ultimate potential. We should aim to become everything we could possibly be. The nifty twist is the idea that rides shotgun: The closer one approaches, the more one's ultimate potential expands.

Thus, the result is a never ending quest for self-improvement, a persistent craving for advancement, and an unyielding mission to upgrade.

Think of it this way: Perhaps I have a goal to become a better disciplinarian. Even though the students are certainly not out of control, it's true that our school has some behavior issues. To address the issue and my relationship to it, I enroll in a workshop titled "Discipline with Dignity." Then, I take action: I attempt to discuss our school rules and behavioral expectations more frequently with the students. Over the course of several months, the overall conduct improves and discipline referrals decrease.

I could stop there, but I don't. I make a concerted effort to spend more time on the grounds before and after school and in the cafeteria during the lunch hour. I walk the halls during passing times, thereby offering more supervision and presence. Now we have even fewer behavior problems, but I know I can help us improve further. I am still looking for a way to connect with our habitual discipline offenders, to interact with them in a positive manner as frequently as possible, to help guide them toward a positive path.

The point is that there's always something *more* I can do. I can always make it *better*. I can always strive to be a better *me*.

The "Always strive to be a better you" maxim, not unlike Commander Bond's, transcends boundaries between work and home, private and public, personal and professional. Ideally, it substantiates a philosophy that we can follow in every aspect of life. One way of viewing it is the pursuit of an ever-elusive quarry, the constant challenge to obtain the unattainable.

When I share this perspective with coworkers, friends, or politicians, I am often asked, "Does this make you feel like the hapless racing greyhound, endlessly chasing that silly fake rabbit?" On the contrary, it leaves me ecstatic with the *pursuit*. I understand and embrace that my quest may never be fulfilled, yet it is the hunt itself that becomes the goal.

Continuous Improvement

The end result is the continuous growth and improvement of *myself*, on all fronts. As I attempt to better myself as a father, brother, soccer coach, supervisor, lecturer, driver, or barbequer; or if I want to be more patient with hostile parents, more understanding with children dealing with trauma, prepare more thoroughly for committee meetings, eliminate sarcasm from my discourse with cantankerous colleagues, or develop ways to deliver more targeted feedback to teachers, my capacity for growth and improvement likewise gain.

This takes dedication, and dedication requires discipline. Discipline, in turn, requires reminders because it's pretty easy to slip back into the ruts of the path already traveled. This mantra is only as effective as it is A) meaningful to me, and B) always on my mind. The answer to charge A is contained herein—the definition and the challenges are explained right here on these pages.

I address part B by repeating, "Always strive to be a better you," or ASTBABY, whenever and wherever I can: The signature on the end of my e-mails allows me to share it with my entire contact list; I've coerced my schools to adopt the philosophy as part of their behavior pledges and discourse; I wear one of those silicone bracelets to provide me a physical and constant reminder of the life I want to lead; I even had the word "strive" tattooed on my shoulder as a permanent aide memoire. This mantra is always on the tip of my tongue, and at the heart of my consciousness.

ASTBABY at Work

My work as the principal of a school demands that I adhere to this philosophy wholeheartedly. Under my daily charge are 600 children and 100 adults; as their leader, I must exhibit strength of character during every interaction, incorruptible integrity even in the most trying times, and the courage of rationality in the face of absurdity. This is when the phrase and the mindset are most useful. I'm sure it's saved my career a couple of times when I've restrained from saying something regrettable and instead pursued the higher road.

The principal must model not perfection, but the *pursuit* of it. I must demonstrate the unyielding desire to improve, and the humbling realities of my weaknesses. I must share the beauty in shunning complacency and tackling the hard work inherent in change. No matter how well things are going right now, I guarantee they're not perfect, ergo, they're not yet good enough. There's room for improvement, and so we must rededicate ourselves toward that end. This is the calling of the job: to push the envelope, to eradicate barriers, to obliterate records, and to redefine excellence.

To me, the principalship is the ultimate post. Though I often consider a switch to international espionage, the calling to manage thousands of children's futures proves too irresistible to ignore. And so as I forge onward, seeking opportunities for continuous growth along every path I tread, I commend my colleagues for making an unmistakable difference. And I urge you: *Always strive to be a better you.*

The Attack

On behalf of the roughly 50 million children in the American public school system, I have a request: I ask you to join me in what I respectfully dub "The Attack." I use the term attack not in the sense of violent fighting, a military assault, or strong criticism. Rather I use it as definition four in the Oxford American Dictionary: to begin vigorous work on.

In today's schools, like in any area of work, things happen. What defines us as educators, as individuals, and as a society is not what happens, but rather how we *respond to* what happens.

Education today has entered an Era of Accountability. We are accountable to the Feds, to the public, and to ourselves, along with higher standards and expectations for all children. There is also growing pressure to prepare our children for global competition, escalating diversity, new technology bombarding us from all sides, and increasing need to address the issues and development of the whole child. We need to respond to these challenges. On the scale of responses, ranging from blind following to indifference, acceptance to questioning, and even challenging, none seems to relay the requisite urgency or recall the appropriate need for action like "attack" does.

What, you may ask, are the targets of our attack?

Attack Illiteracy First

Our children need, more than anything, to learn the basic literacy skills of reading, writing, and communicating. Even if we ignore for a moment that literacy is the cornerstone of every assessment program in America, think of the children's dire need to have those skills for the rest of their lives. Think of the written portion of the driver's license test, job applications, placement tests, medical forms, crossword puzzles . . . I could go on ad infinitum.

Certainly each of us knows an individual who is functionally illiterate, and our hearts break at the idea of his struggles. In fact, according to the 2003 National Assessment of Adult Literacy, only thirteen percent of American adults possess reading abilities in the proficient range (check out www.nces.ed.gov for more amazing statistics). That's roughly one in every eight. If that doesn't get your attention, you could use another semester in Statistics 101.

At the school level, we can change that. *You* can change that. Dedicate your school to the teaching and learning of literacy; focus your discussions and budgets on literacy needs; give literacy instruction the time it requires and then add a little more; and teach new teachers how to teach reading.

Attack the Status Quo

The quote, "The mark of insanity is doing the same thing over and over again and expecting different results," is attributed to Albert Einstein.

The definition of status quo is "the state of affairs as it is," according to the Oxford American Dictionary.

As educators, and as members of a greater society, it should be clear to us that our output is insufficient. The data do not lie: We have thousands of schools nationwide facing sanctions for underperformance; we are facing an epidemic of childhood obesity and health issues; we are in danger of short-sheeting our children's education in favor of numerous tests and shallow content.

The output data being clear, it is also clear that our input must be likewise insufficient. Argue for change, rock the boat, shake the tree. Greatness and growth are borne from change. In fact, they are intimately linked together. Change is the very nature of this business, so go create, innovate, contribute.

I share with you my mantra: *Always strive to be a better you.* This philosophy necessarily requires change, for it is a prerequisite for improvement.

Attack the Achievement Gap

There is no reason that every child in America cannot achieve at proficient and outstanding rates. Our poor and minority children are just as capable of succeeding and flourishing when given the same opportunities and exposure to the highest-quality instruction and rigorous educational experiences as our white and more advantaged students.

There are enough examples of schools achieving comparable proficiency rates to question why white eighth grade students scored 26 points higher than their African-American counterparts in literary proficiency. We must attack the reality that on the National Assessment of Educational Progress (NAEP), the data haven't changed since 1998, the gap hasn't lessened—and it's the same for our Latino students.

We can do better, and every American child, in every American school, deserves better. There should be no ceiling atop anyone's dreams, and there should be no ceiling lowering anyone's potential.

Attack Apathy

How many of us have witnessed a colleague, a professional educator, throw up his or her hands and lament the circumstances of "these kids," the lack of parental involvement, the dearth of funding, the unmotivated youth of today, or some such hogwash, using it as justification for an inability to do the job? It has been said that, "he who is good at complaining is likely not much use for anything else." What do we do when we hear a teacher say, "I just teach—they'll either get it or they won't"? Our inaction serves as fuel for the perpetuation of this destructive apathy.

Take heed to the words of Thomas Jefferson: "Determine never to be idle . . . It is wonderful how much may be done if we are always doing."

Light fires to stimulate your colleagues. Refuse to accept excuses for underperformance. Don't just stand there. Get involved! I believe that's why we're in the business of education: because we care enough to act.

Attack Mediocrity

Let's not celebrate accomplishments that aren't adequately earned. Let's not allow the standards to be lowered just so that more students can be labeled "proficient." Lowered expectations just beget lowered performance, and then we congratulate ourselves for making the mark? I think not.

"Okay" is not good enough. A shrug of the shoulders is as effective as a day spent ill in bed. The educational experiences of our children need rigor, and our standards need relevance. Raise the bar, expect more, shoot for the stars—we all have greatness within us, and every child has limitless potential. Draw it out of them, and demand no less than excellence.

All told, what we say means very little. Words without deeds mean nothing unless we act appropriately upon them. What we do matters greatly. And where is most of the "doing" done? In our schools, in our classrooms, in our school boards, in our district offices, in our universities, and in our homes.

As we embark upon a new school year, created with equal parts anticipation and trepidation, we must heed the call and corral our mighty forces. Our children deserve a united front. So, again I ask you to join me in the battle. Join the attack.

Leading Off the Edge of the Map

Remember Rowlf the Dog from the Muppet Show? Sure, you have images of Miss Piggy, Kermit the Frog, and Fozzie Bear bouncing freely in your memory bank, but no Rowlf the Dog? He may not have been your most favorite Muppet, but now that I've mentioned him, you have to admit he was one heck of a piano player.

Why, when tickling the ivories prior to singing, "I Hope That Something Better Comes Along" with Kermit in 1979's *The Muppet Movie*, he humbly accepts the Frog's praise by saying, "I'm no Heifetz, but I get by."

Pick a Heifetz, Any Heifetz

Rowlf was referring to Jascha Heifetz, the Russian-born violin prodigy. This is not the same Heifetz as Ronald A. Heifetz, who in 1994 penned *Leadership Without Easy Answers* (Harvard University Press), but there's a connection in here somewhere, I just know it, so stick with me.

In reading Ronald's investigation into a definition of the term "leadership" that takes values into account, I came upon a reference he made to Sidney Hook's 1943 *The Hero in History*, in which Hook claims, "some men are eventful, while others are event-making."

History shines a light on event-makers. For some, it's a spotlight, illuminating the great and wondrous innovations produced by a person of action. For others, it's the single dangling 100-watt bulb of a damp interrogation room, demanding explanation for unwarranted deeds. Either way, event-makers make history and, in the end, we're all just history, aren't we?

By the way, who invented the electric light bulb? That's correct: Thomas Edison.[1] And who *didn't* invent the light bulb? Correct again: Every other unnamed person on the face of the earth. Who do you remember? Who does history favor, then? Thrice correct: The event-maker.

---

[1]Lesser-known fact: Edison didn't actually invent the first electric light bulb; he fixed errors in others' attempts and made the first commercially produced electric light bulb that worked consistently. But he is rightly remembered for his innovations.

Uncharted Waters

At the risk of inundating you with Cliff Clavinesque facts, wasn't it Ferdinand Magellan[2] who first circumnavigated the globe in 1519–1521? This Portuguese explorer had devised a plan, refused to accept "no" as an answer, and leapt forward to carry it out. He was an event-maker.

To relate this to the principalship, sometimes the best course of action is one that no one has ever taken before. Our students' new and varied needs scream for a divergent approach. Sometimes it's okay to shun the status quo. In fact, there are times that it's preferable, in the name of growth and progress, to ignore what everyone else is doing. In fact, some moments appear before us, begging us to obliterate that old standby (the status quo, not *The Muppet Movie*) and to forge a new path. Into the mysterious unknown we go!

As school principals, often where we lead is off the edge of the map. Captain Barbossa[3] (from Disney's *Pirates of the Caribbean*) may warn us, "Here there be monsters," but our quest for excellence must know no bounds. We must be willing to excuse ourselves from the masses and serve as pioneers, breaking ground and cutting waves. This is where breakthroughs lie, this is where obstacles are overcome, this is where questions are answered, and this is where excellence awaits.

Make It Happen

History will reward the event-makers, and as principals we have a choice to make: Will we react to the events of yesterday, or will we make the events of tomorrow? Certainly, one might argue that this is a pursuit of glory, of achievement, and the garnishment of superlatives. But what argument for glory

---

[2]Magellan, sadly, did not complete the globe's first circumnavigation, either. We remember his name for this feat, even though he died on the trek and didn't see it to completion. Some of his original crew, however, did make the entire journey, carrying his torch as a vanguard.

[3]As a word of caution: Any time you heed a warning from a fictional character from a wildly popular film, take a break, make yourself a quesadilla, get a haircut . . . and then get back to your work. It's apparent that you need some reality grounding.

ever began with a reference to a floppy-eared, mild-mannered puppet?

No, this is an argument for turning over every stone—in fact, sailing far from the beaten path just to find additional stones to turn over—in order to discover what works for every individual child. In schools, the status quo is often silently revered. We do as was done unto us, even if that original doing was done decades before and we really ought to know better by now.

In recent years, we've learned so much about the way young people learn, about the way brains process information, and about instructional pedagogy that we'd be remiss to ignore it. Unfortunately, the status quo is often a decade or two (or ten) behind. Are we truly providing what our students deserve if we turn a blind eye to the best, most recent, and most promising information? How long can we stifle our inner excellence?

New results require new action. New action demands new learning. New learning insists upon new thought. So go ahead—think off the map, weigh your options, and create a plan. (A plan, mind you, is not the same as shooting from the hip; a plan indicates a certain level of forethought and understanding.) Make it happen. History rewards the event-makers among us.

As for the Heifetz connection: Jascha, a violin virtuoso who wowed audiences for over 60 years, sought perfection at every turn. Ronald could have studied Jascha for lessons in leadership: Part of what compelled Jascha's incessant desire for perfection was his self-admitted "horror of mediocrity."

Rowlf the Dog, meanwhile, just got by.

Get Bent: Hell-Bent

Ring the nearest bell if this scenario sounds familiar: You're at a meeting.

Wait, no, don't ring the bell just yet! Let me finish setting the scene for you. I know you're in education and you've been diagnosed with a slowly growing malignant mass in your psyche, eating away at your enthusiasm and energy like a parasitic traffic jam. It's called meetingitis, and it's common, but let's get our bearings first.

So you're at a meeting. It's a brainstorming/planning meeting at which you and your colleagues are tossing out some fantastic ideas to address a very real and very serious issue. Following the team-meeting protocol, you've jotted down a diverse and impressive list of possible actions, then you engage in a thought-and-debate-provoking activity that results in the creation of a shorter, prioritized list. The team is jazzed. These strategies just might be the answer to all our heartaches. The buzz is palpable. But then . . .

The team leader, maybe it's you, says, "Okay, folks. Let's look at action item number one. We need a 'project manager' to oversee the implementation of this strategy. Who's going to take this one on?" That's when the nervousness begins, and the buzz dissipates. The jazz wanes. Confident enthusiasm quickly turns to the shuffling of papers as the team members refuse resolutely to make eye contact with the team leader. All of a sudden everyone's shoelaces are untied.

We all agree the ideas are rock solid. We all concur that action item number one requires our attention. We all have an accord that it would do our school, district, or department good to move in this direction, and move quickly. But, "I can't, I'm swamped," is the only chorus filling the airwaves.

That's the end of the scenario. Does it sound familiar? I hear bells ringing. Lots of bells.

We've all got excuses to NOT be the project managers. These projects take time. They require energy. They need attention. We're all swamped. We're all overworked, underpaid, over-stressed, and the fact that we walk uphill five miles in the snow to work (and then home again) goes unappreciated. But these are good ideas. They're rock solid, remember? They could make a world of difference to us as professionals, to our students, their families, their futures, and to our communities. We can't just leave them on the table, can we?

Somewhere out there is a graveyard of good initiatives. Buried in unmarked tombs are scores of brilliant suggestions, some of them written on giant sticky Post-It notes with Sharpie markers, some typed into a Microsoft Word document, some of them scribbled on napkins with the "O'Henry's Go-Go Bar" logo in the corner. I'd like to visit that vast cemetery some day, to pay my respects, to inter a couple of lofty plans that went nowhere faster than Nike's forgotten Concrete Cross-Training line, and to dig up a couple dozen ideas that I could take back to my own teams.

I'd take those crumpled up pieces of paper, those notebooks with cat-scratches in the margins, and those discarded flash-drives, and scour them for diamonds. And then, when I present them to my team, I'd follow our protocol, offer a ridiculously powerful, emotional, and logical argument to implement it, and then I'd close with these powerful words: "Team, let's get bent . . .

"Hell-Bent!"

Some call it "being gung-ho." Others claim it's "initiative." More say it's "ownership." Maybe it's "fired up," "getting behind it," or "carrying the torch." Whatever moniker it answers to, the element of this phenomenon that we're so often lacking, and that we're so desperately needing, is having someone—anyone—hell-bent enough to bring our fantastic idea to fruition. Someone needs to step up and take on the role of project manager.

Think of the greatest innovations that were successfully implemented in schools. Consider some of the strongest suggestions that were effectively enacted in business. Ponder some of the most impactful actions that were triumphantly carried out in our society. Each of these was thought up by someone, most likely in a brainstorming committee with donuts and generic coffee. But more importantly, each was also acted upon by a change agent like a project manager. Someone, folks, was hell-bent enough to make it happen.

Some schools opt to run single-gender classes. Others have every teacher present every lesson using GLAD (Guided Language Acquisition and Development) strategies, even though few students in the classroom are second-language learners. Many have embraced the Professional Learning Communities concept and have organized their once Lone-Rangeresque staff members into functioning teams. Great strategies needn't be earth-shattering, either. They can be as simple as committing to a fundraiser, implementing a parent newsletter, launching an after-school tutoring program, writing a grant, or creating a mid-term assessment.

All sorts of fantastic things are happening out there, but they didn't just materialize out of the blue. They were imagined, envisioned, suggested, considered, disputed, revised, adopted. Then, someone with true vision and gusto climbed aboard that bull, grabbed it by the scruff of the neck and led the charge à la William Wallace into battle.

It was Leonardo da Vinci who said, "People of accomplishment rarely sat back and let things happen to them. They went out and happened to things." Michael Jordan, more of a contemporary to most of us, followed with this logic: "Some people *want* it to happen, some *wish* it would happen, others *make* it happen."

When it comes time to take that great idea and put it into place, what will be your strategy? Will you sit back and let world-changing propositions die, only to be tossed haphazardly into a coffin and sent six feet under? Will you create an environment that welcomes initiative, rewards gumption, and celebrates leadership? And when push comes to shove, will you rise up, stand in front of your team and behind the idea, and accept the challenges of breathing life into it? Will you get bent—hell-bent?

Why 100 Percent Matters

An elementary school in Washington State recently set itself a ridiculously haughty goal of having 100 percent of its students represented by a parent during the semi-annual parent-teacher conferences. That school, receiving Title I funding for its high-poverty clientele and carting a rather respectable history of 90 percent attendance at such meetings, embraced the challenge of meeting with an adult in every single child's life and refused to settle for anything less.

One of the most passionately debated topics of 21st Century education surrounds the primary tenet of the No Child Left Behind (NCLB) Act: All students, and that means 100 percent of enrolled students, will test at or above proficiency levels by the 2013–2014 school year. That is, most all of us will agree, quite a hill to climb.

Advocates of accountability insist that high standards for all students are necessary to promote academic growth and spur achievement to levels heretofore unseen. Proponents of the "whole child" claim such goals are ill-conceived and detract from our true mission in school: to prepare each student, as an individual, to meet his or her own potential. And both are right, aren't they?

Inevitably, into the debate struts the number 100. There it is, masquerading as both the lofty goal and the pie-in-the-sky rhetoric, with a percent sign following it. Just the thought of 100 percent of our students reaching proficiency tingles our spines and quirks our eyebrows. In many corners of many back-yard barbeques and hotel lobbies, educators and noneducators alike have debated the merits of this NCLB goal. Described as "achievable," "ridiculous," "impossible," and "haughty," 100 percent is nonetheless the standard against which we compare everything education-related.

Forget for a moment the sanctions, the funding issues, and the achievement gap. Though those are all worth mentioning, they are merely asides in this theater. Let's consider that number, 100.

Around the year 100 C.E., lions became extinct in Europe. 100 is also:

♦ the number of years in a century
♦ the sum of the first nine prime numbers (just add up $2 + 3 + 5 + 7 + 11 + 13 + 17 + 19 + 23$)
♦ the Periodic Table address for fermium (atomic number 100)
♦ the emergency response number in Israel
♦ the temperature to heat water to in degrees Celsius if you want it to boil
♦ commonly referred to as the *perfect square* of a *perfect ten*

Perfect

Pardon all that rambling. Its sole purpose was to get me to the concept of *perfect*. One hundred percent of anything is a perfect whole. The entirety of something. Completeness. The absence of absence, if you will. Perfection.

That Washington elementary school's goal seemed like a good idea at the time, but it also carried the burden of additional responsibilities, extra stress for staff, and undoubtedly longer hours and more pressure. While illuminated and noble, it wasn't immediately embraced. It was a struggle from the start.

In the end, about 80 percent obliged quite willingly. Phone calls and notes home coerced the next ten percent to cross the threshold. Then it was do-or-die time for the ten percent who were left. The teaching staff had already called, already sent home notes, already e-mailed, already offered rewards to students, and already pulled out their thinning hair. This final ten percent would be the steepest part of the hill to climb. Would it be worth the effort?

Who would argue with the results they'd already attained? 90 percent is a pretty big, impressive number all by itself. Not all professional basketball players hit 90 percent of their foul shots, and they're so easy that they're called "free" throws. But a 90 percent goal is inherently exclusionary; it chops ten percent off, right from the get-go. It sends a message, philosophical or otherwise, that not everyone is worthy, and that our expectations have limits. We don't need to, nor are we committed to, reaching every single one of our children. But that's not okay.

Who Are the Final Ten Percent?

We all know the answer to that question. Quite plainly, the final ten percent are the ones we need to meet most. They are the parents of the children with the most pressing needs, the most dire circumstances, the highest risk for future failure, the greatest prevalence of behavior issues, the most common occurrence of _____ (you fill in the blank because you know who those children are!), and *they* need *us* the most.

So, having exhausted all the resources they had used in the past, the teaching staff upped the ante. Teachers began to accompany students home. They stayed after school until 6:00 p.m. when the parents came to pick their kids up from the after-school program. They called home during the evening. They left hundreds of messages. They even visited parents at work. They did, in short, *whatever it took.* They were relentless in their pursuit of the goal—not for the goal's sake, but for the kids' sake. They were going to meet with that final ten percent of parents.

When the mother of child #600 (out of 600) arrived at the school office to drop off the student's medication before heading back to the local shelter, the assistant principal sprinted to cover the teacher's classroom so she could meet face-to-face with the mother.

It was, by all accounts, a beautiful scene. 100 percent, including that all-important final ten percent. You might call it the *perfect* ten percent. The results of all that commotion to meet with every child's parents were twofold:

First, it allowed the teaching staff to get a handle on every single child on campus by opening up authentic communication between the school and home, by sharing valuable information, and by outlining current progress and concerns.

Second, it taught that staff a very important lesson: Any goal, no matter how lofty and unattainable it may have seemed, was achievable if they were willing to work together, to think creatively about solutions, and to act with a relentless tenacity previously witnessed only in pre-100 C.E. European lions.

Think about it. It's perfect.

Hope Ain't a Strategy

You know how some words have double meanings? Sometimes they confuse us if we're not paying attention, like when your brother sets you up on a blind date and says, "She has a really nice personality," or idioms like, "It's raining cats and dogs out there," which befuddle most three-year-olds. Well, what I'm referring to are real words that have double meanings. In particular, in my meanderings through the Oxford Unabridged

Dictionary and historical presidential inaugurations, I've stumbled across the word **hope**.

As a noun, hope is a beautiful thing. It's what we all hold onto when we think about the future, about our children, our country, and our favorite baseball teams. Hope is the proverbial light at the end of the tunnel, beckoning us with some sort of promise that our lot will improve. It is the beacon of children's dreams, manifested by caring and demanding educators, navigating the treacherous waters of reality, and showing them the course from here to there. Hope as a noun gives us energy to continue, to fight, to work, and to persevere.

As a verb, hope is okay at best. We can hope the neighbor's dog will stop barking in the middle of the night. We can hope that our hair doesn't fall out before our next high school reunion. Maybe hoping makes us feel better when we're confronted with elements of our life that are beyond our control.

However, as a strategy in schools, hope just doesn't belong. Quite simply, hope is not a strategy. Think about how silly it would be to rewrite your school's mission statement this way: "The mission of Mountain View Middle School is to hope our kids learn to read, write, and do arithmetic so they can be prepared for a variety of pursuits in our diverse and democratic society."

However, to a certain extent, hope is still a prevalent approach in our schools, our classrooms, and our boardrooms across the country. We hope our students will pass the state tests. We hope our troubled children will grow out of their problematic behaviors. We hope our slower children will catch up. We hope all of our students will grasp the lesson objectives and learn the material. We hope the colleges will invite and accept every young person we churn out. We hope our teachers will pursue their own professional development. We hope education salaries rise to a parallel with sanitation workers and airline pilots. We hope . . .

. . . but what are we *doing* about it?

Taking Action

Rather than simply throwing hope onto the table, let's take some responsibility for our situation. Encourage your teachers to *expect* their students to master their spelling words and to enroll in AP classes. *Expect* that your staff will work tirelessly to communicate the learning objectives and utilize formative assessments in your building. *Expect* that your students will demonstrate compassion for others and exhibit exemplary citizenship. Let's throw down the gauntlet here instead:

Change something. The next time you find yourself in a meeting with teachers and you overhear "I sure hope he learns to be more responsible before he gets to high school," ask instead, "What are we going to do to help him learn responsibility?" We can't sit back and watch a student flail—hoping alone is indefensible—when we can brainstorm some interventions and put them into place. When it's not working, we've got to change something and try anew.

Set goals immediately. Once we identify what we're hoping for, we've got the main raw ingredient for a goal. Then all we need to do is dissect the goal, break it down into reasonable short-term targets, and get to work climbing the staircase to accomplish it. Every time we hear somebody mutter something about "hoping such-and-such happens," we should immediately spin that around by saying, "Excellent! You've identified a goal. Let's get to work making it happen." The longer we wait, the less likely we are to set the goal, start our work toward it, make progress, or celebrate its accomplishment. So do it now.

Act intentionally. Now that we've determined that an element of our school needs a change and we've framed the ideal situation as a goal, it's time to make a list of precise strategies and try one out. What is a specific intervention that we can attempt that will most likely yield a benefit? Start it today, implement the strategy for a designated period of time, collect data, and revisit to compare our progress with our benchmark targets. Just don't shoot from the hip—be intentional. Goals in and of themselves are only as effective as the strategies we implement to accomplish them. And to meet those standards, we must take actions *on purpose*.

Hope is not a bad thing, not by a long shot. Hope carries with it the power of optimism. But using hope as a strategy for school improvement? That will never work because elements of schooling really *are* within our control. We, as educators, have tremendous power to reach out and *do* something to help those in need. What's more, we have the obligation to do so. In order to make a difference, we cannot watch blithely as our schools unravel and our children's potential goes unfulfilled. The time is now.

I sure *hope* you've paid attention. Scratch that: I *expect* you're going to make a difference.

The True Beauty of Goals

Everybody likes statistics these days, so I'm going to start us off with some figures that will blow your mind. These are stats about goal-setting, and they're not confined to education. They're global:

- If you do not set a goal, the likelihood that you achieve your goal sits at roughly 0%.
- Just the act of setting a goal raises the odds of success to 19.7%.
- Writing down your goal and keeping it somewhere you can refer to it frequently jumps your likelihood of achievement to 45.5%.
- Sharing your goal with someone who can hold you accountable to it pops you up to 51.2%.
- All that plus identifying and pursuing specific action steps and engaging in honest self-reflection elevates your potential for reaching your goal all the way up to 86.1%!

Think about it from the perspective of weight loss, a topic usually brought up twice a year: as a New Year's resolution and right before bathing suit season begins. You'll start by looking in the mirror and lamenting, "Good lord, who stuffed the marshmallows into my body? Is that a circus mirror? I'm upset with my body image, and now my belt must have gotten wet, shrank, and doesn't fit any more. Jeesh." Just thinking those thoughts won't help you lose any weight, will they? You're at 0%.

Let's say that, as a result of your negative self-talk and your desire to wear that new suit (bathing or otherwise), you set a goal to lose 15 pounds. That's terrific—we could all shed a few here or there. Now, for about one in every five people, that'll do it.

You write your goal on a 3 × 5 card and tape it to your bathroom mirror (though a smarter idea would be to post it on your fridge and by the snack bar at work). You're almost halfway there. A coworker sets a similar goal, and the two of you decide to track your progress and keep the other honest in working toward the goal. You've crossed the threshold.

One night, after watching a particularly inspiring episode of "The Biggest Loser," you find yourself truly committed to the goal. You schedule four swim workouts a week with your coworker, all at 5:00 a.m., which is much earlier than you would dare to get up by yourself. You throw out the junk food from your pantry. You write down weekly check-in events to measure your progress, to celebrate your successes, and to recalibrate your efforts. You're on the right track now!

Singer and comedian Todd Snider claims that, "64 percent of all the world's statistics are made up right there on the spot . . . and 82.4 percent of people believe 'em whether they're accurate statistics or not." I'm not sure if that is accurate, and you're probably wondering where I got my figures anyway, but the most important thing to remember is that this is all based on a powerful blend of common sense, research, and experience. And I went to college as a statistics major, so trust me on this.

Big, Smart Goals

Goals hold a prominent spot in the educational landscape. We set goals for reducing the dropout rate, increasing the graduation rate, decreasing the number of nonproficient students in any given subcategory on the annual standardized test, or increasing the students enrolled in AP classes. We've learned and can chant the SMART acronym: Specific, Measureable, Attainable, Results-oriented, and Time-bound. We've bounced between exclusionary goals ("85% of students will pass the end-of-course exam in all math and science classes this semester," for example—that's exclusionary because if we meet it, we've still left 15 percent out in the cold) and all-inclusive goals ("100 percent of students will make over a year's growth in reading level by March 31 of this school year," for example—that involves every child). We've had goals set for us (does "100 percent by 2014" sound familiar?) and we've been asked to set them ourselves.

How do we decide which goals to set? Lower goals are easier to reach, but loftier goals indicate our belief in potential . . . and we're rewarded that much more when we achieve them. Steven Farr, of Teach For America, dedicates an entire chapter to the idea of "Big Goals" in his realistic and inspirational book, *Teaching as Leadership*. In it, he chronicles wildly successful teachers that took extremely challenging environments, set ambitious all-inclusive goals, and proceeded to realize absurd triumphs. How did they do it, you ask? And, more importantly, how can you do it? Read on:

A Goal-Setting Game Plan

Step 1: Set a relevant goal. The goal must mean something to you, either personally or professionally. Do you see yourself in the goal, either contributing to it or benefiting from its completion? Are you clear on what you want to accomplish? Check it against the SMART criteria: "90 percent of our students will pass each math end-of-course assessment" is a more effective (specific, measurable, attainable, results-oriented, and time-bound) goal than "All of our students will be better prepared for middle school," because we have a better idea of exactly what we're trying to achieve.

Step 2: Write your goal in positive language. How will you feel when you meet it? Link it to a positive emotion. Dr. Edwin Locke's 1968 article, "Toward a Theory of Task Motivation and Incentives," described the link between goals and motivation. If we have goals that we're working toward, we'll be more motivated to achieve them. Suggested phrasing: "I am proud that 90 percent of my students are passing the end-of-unit math exams." Reaching that level of proficiency brings pride; working toward that pride brings motivation.

Step 3: Clarify your strategies. Hall of Fame UCLA basketball coach John Wooden, in his book, *Wooden on Leadership*, makes the case: "Often we place such emphasis on distant goals that inadequate attention is given to what it takes to get there—the day-by-day particulars of how you conduct business." So let's attend to the details, shall we? Identify three to five specific action steps/strategies that you can commit to that'll lead you toward your goal. In the "90 percent math goal" scenario presented above, that might mean teaching only to clearly identified learning objectives, providing review activities three times a week, offering lunchtime tutoring support to struggling students, and calling parents with suggestions for study habits. It takes specific action steps to realize success, or to make progress at all. Without strategies, goals are just pipe dreams, castles in the air, lipstick on pigs.

Step 4: Dedicate some time to reflect. Spencer Johnson, M.D. calls this step "affirmations" or "feeling the fumble" in his book *The One-Minute Teacher*. We can call it celebrations and calibrations. Use frequent reflection periods (daily if you can, weekly at least) as benchmark assessments for yourself: If you're truly engaging in the strategies you've identified, give yourself a high-five. Nice work, good job, you're on track, keep it up! If you've been slipping, you've got to make yourself *feel* bad . . . temporarily. You've been sloppy, this isn't working, you're headed for disaster. Then recalibrate: Okay, this is meaningful work, the strategies are solid, and you can get yourself back on track starting right now! Dr. Locke referred to "feedback," and in this case I suggest you provide yourself the feedback through self-reflection. If possible, seek out a workout partner who will share honest feedback with you, someone who will help keep you honest and accountable.

With concerted effort, working toward relevant goals by defining them, putting them in positive language, implementing concrete strategies, reflecting often, and meeting attainable benchmarks along the way will take us to remarkable heights. The only limit on our goals is our own commitment. Rather than wallowing through another Bathing Suit Season wearing a bedsheet, join the 64.8 percent of the population that's embraced a SMARTer goal-setting structure. Now that's a statistic you can get behind!

Ten Lessons I've Learned from My Students

Here I was, thinking—as the principal of a 500-student elementary school—that I was in charge of the instruction occurring within our walls. I was scrutinizing the teachers' lesson delivery; strengthening the implementation of curriculum and informative assessments; building capacity through professional development, intentionality of best-practice teaching, and relentless self-reflection; and ensuring that every student had access to the highest-quality instruction on this side of Pluto.

Then it hit me.

Education isn't just one way. It, like most avenues of life, travels with reciprocity. Even as the principal, the Chief Everything Officer and Instructional Leader, I found myself simultaneously astonished and inspired at the lessons delivered to me by the very students to whom I've pledged to deliver lessons.

Every decade is special. The 1770s were full of revolutionaries and Freedom Fighters. The 1870s brought us the first cable cars in San Francisco. The 1970s had bell-bottom pants and disco music. The end of the 2010–2011 school year marked my tenth in school administration, so I thought I'd wax poetic a little bit as I stroll down memory lane.

However, like the Roman god Janus, I'll maintain my forward vision as I'm peering back. Today, while I reminisce about the last eventful decade, I will scrutinize the lessons taught to me by the students I've known so that our future endeavors in the principalship might yield even better, stronger, more consistent results.

What follows is but a sampling; I'd encourage you to record your own.

1. Never give up. I was cussed at, spat upon, shoved, insulted, threatened, and told I have pointy elf-ears, all by a 12-year-old boy named Marcos. Nevertheless, it was my responsibility—my obligation, actually—to remain steadfastly professional, respectful, and optimistic, so I sought deep to see the talents and gifts of this student. Beneath the bullying exterior was an intelligent, athletic little boy who was destined to be a leader. Keeping a strengths-based view allowed Marcos to stay in school, to eventually turn that scowl into a smile, and to become a leader on his high school track and field team. Without the consistent support and chances to be successful, he may have become a "coulda-been" drop-out.

2. Nothing works for everyone. Exceptions prove the rule, don't they? Whether we're talking about behavior plans, lesson delivery, classroom management, assessments, extracurricular events, or even daily schedules, it's important to consider the individual students' strengths, tendencies, goals, and motivations. Let's allow Danielle to stand during circle time since she's antsy; let's permit Conner to doodle in his journal during a lecture because it actually helps him listen; let's sanction Barney's 15-minute break every hour because it will allow him to refocus and be more productive during the next 45 minutes. Though each of those actions violates the school rule, the exceptions are necessary for the individual child in question.

3. We've got two ears, too. We need to listen to our kids. A student named Michelle used to be a chronic castaway from the library because she refused to sit down for the read-aloud. The teacher gave her the obligatory three chances, then sent her away for being disobedient. Upon arrival in the office, she'd accept her punishments with a scowl and sadly count the days until the next library class. It turned out that Michelle had a bone condition that prevented her from sitting on the floor for extended periods of time, yet her teacher had never allowed her the opportunity to explain herself. Once the teacher learned about Michelle's condition, a simple solution presented itself: She could sit in a chair on the fringe of the group. Without intending to do so, we were damaging this girl's love of stories and learning because we hadn't listened.

4. Relationships, relationships, relationships. I heard a good quote the other day: "They won't care to learn until we learn to care." I'm not sure who gets credit for it, so I'll leave it at that. Nevertheless, I had a young man named George who came to his teacher one year with a tremendous reputation for being a troublemaker. He spent the majority of the year as a troublemaker, and had conflict after conflict with his hapless teacher. They had never bonded and built the rapport necessary for George to create his own sense of efficacy. Before considering a move to a more restrictive behavior-intensive program, we moved George to a neighboring classroom with a teacher he respected and who returned that respect. George turned over a new leaf and flourished because of high expectations, a sense of effort-optimism, and a strong teacher–student relationship.

5. It takes a village. I used to think it was my responsibility to reach just one student in a deep, profound, grasshopper manner. Then I sought to reach them all. Well, to the old me I say, "Good luck, pardner!" Relinquish control. It's not just you, the principal, who makes a big difference. Every child needs an adult, but not always the CEO. If I have trouble relating to a particular student, but another adult has a magnificent bond with the student, fantastic! If I don't have any ideas to support Althea's learning goals, but a team of six staff members comes together and brainstorms a plan that will work, wonderful! They're *our* children, not just mine and not just yours.

6. Set goals. Without a goal, we're just meandering down the river of life paddling for the sake of paddling. If we don't know where we're going, we'll never know when we get there, and we'll be awfully tired and grumpy along the way. Katie, a first grader, took one look at an end-of-first-grade reading passage and crossed her arms defiantly. She said she'd never read all those words, but when we divided the words into more manageable portions and set short-term goals, she met them easily! She was reading like a second grader by the time the snow melted in April.

7. Attend to the Whole Child. I worked with a fourth-grade girl named Lori who was a miserable student, full of self-doubt, and whose shyness made her difficult to approach socially. She struggled in school and struggled with making friends. Academic tasks had no meaning and she began to spiral downward. Then we had a special performance of a dance troupe, and they asked Lori to join them on stage, in front of our entire student body, for a dance-off. Shy, uncomfortable little Lori sprang to life before our very eyes. Oh, could that child move! From then on, she beamed as classmates recalled her skills and poise, and she began to connect with peers and, subsequently, academics. What if we had noted that skill earlier in her school career? Could we have staved off her insecurities and tapped into her esteem?

8. Simple is good. We sometimes think the most sophisticated computer games, the most elaborate playground structures, and the most otherworldly activities are the answer for our students' TV-like five-minute attention spans. Foster, a fifth-grader, is one of many I've seen who can sit under a giant tree, pick at the dirt with a stick, and pretend to unearth fossils of creatures from yesteryear. I've had a group of 20 play soccer with a broken chunk of a bike helmet when I lost the ball-shed key. Countless students have figured out how to slash and jab at each other with invisible light sabers. Abraham Lincoln, not one of my students, learned to write by scratching coal on the smooth side of a shovel. Creativity and imagination are our friends, and we ought to encourage them.

9. Laugh. What are our faces telling those around us if they aren't smiling? One particularly rough day, when the disciplinary issues seemed never-ending, the teachers were grumpy as Oscar the Grouch. I must have been seething and fuming down the hallway when a first-grader stopped me and asked, "Mr. Hall, are you mad?" I didn't answer right away, but then said, "Well, yes, actually I am." Then he replied, innocently, "Is that why your face and your socks turned red?"

We all have a Marcos, a Danielle, a Foster, a _____ (you fill in the name), and each has a story. How do we view them? What lessons are they teaching us? How can we use those lessons to turn a profit (in human capital) in our high-stakes educational system? Those lessons, and all that follow, take us to the most essential lesson . . .

10. Always strive to be a better you. What did you expect? The time is now. Let's learn our lessons.

Reviving the American Dream

In my career, I have worked in a variety of different schools in a variety of different settings. I've worked in preschool, elementary school, and middle school institutions. Though the bulk of my work has been concentrated in high-poverty neighborhoods, I've also tread the grass on the other side of the fence. And, of course, I've gotten splinters from trying to uproot the fence and replant it elsewhere.

Recently, a growing number of my conversations and experiences are leading my thoughts in a direction that, quite honestly, disturbs me. I'm wrought with concern over the vitality of that enigmatic ideal we've dubbed "The American Dream."

My concerns about the American Dream relate directly to the very children we have pledged to educate and prepare for the world, as well as their families, teachers, and other members of our communities.

The State of Affairs

In recent months, I've been reading a lot about society, changes in the world, and the future awaiting our children. I've dog-eared pages in Ruby Payne's discussion of poverty, Jonathan Kozol's latest tirades, and some interesting commentaries from the Wall Street Journal—including Jeffrey Zaslow's ire-inspiring column, "Blame it on Mr. Rogers" (WSJ, July 5, 2007).

The same questions Mr. Zaslow attempts to answer have been bopping around my head and have entered my discussions with educators around the country: Are we praising children undeservedly? Are children today more narcissistic than in the past? Have we forgotten to teach children proper citizenship behaviors? Have we ignored our responsibility to instill respect in them? Are we over-indulgent with our children? Was the self-esteem movement of the 1980s a damaging influence?

In a lot of cases, those questions are followed by sadly affirmative responses. What do we see in schools today? In society? Complacency. Lack of drive. Poor efforts. Entitlement. Big egos. Underachievement. Sloppy work. Messy backpacks. Disrespect. Selfishness. An unnatural obsession with the Paris Hiltons of the world. The list could go on . . .

What Is the American Dream?

The United States of America was founded on a few basic principles—self-evident truths, if you will—including the unalienable right to life, liberty, the pursuit of happiness, and the dream of a Boston Red Sox World Series championship (mind you, that is not in the Declaration of Independence). It was those truths that provided the foundation for what James Truslow Adams first coined "The American Dream" in his 1931 book *The Epic of America.*

As citizens of the great U.S.A., we often argue about the true meaning of "The American Dream." Are we talking about the hope of a better standard of living? The dream of a fuller and richer life? The pursuit of greater financial prosperity? The desire of a happier and more peaceful existence? The expectation of enhanced freedoms for all people? The hope of a funnier lineup of Thursday night television programming?

I'm a firm believer in a comprehensive definition of the American Dream: A life that holds the fullest opportunity for any and all of the above.

Continuous Improvement

Go back up two paragraphs and reread the comparative adjectives. You'll find words such as *better, fuller, richer, greater, happier, more peaceful, enhanced,* and *funnier.* Implied in the use of those terms is that in order to achieve the American Dream, we must strive for improvement. The American Dream that I'm referring to has nothing to do with socioeconomic status, race, political affiliation, or shoe size. Instead, it has everything to do with individual and collective gains; gains in freedom, peace, prosperity, happiness, spirituality, opportunity, education, patience, and more.

The half-million immigrants who become naturalized U.S. citizens every year, like the immigrants before them (including our Founding Fathers), have usually had a *clear* picture of the gains they expect to realize. And I'm almost certain that all those who crossed the Atlantic in ships' holds en route to Ellis Island weren't thinking of what they had to lose from failing—only what they had to gain from succeeding.

Today, as in the past, immigrants come to our country in search of their American Dreams. In short, and however they might define it, their goal is a better life. It's not that their lives right now are so bad. They simply want *better*. Heck, most of us probably feel we have pretty good lives, but that doesn't stop us from wanting them to be better. I want it better for my children. I want them to have the opportunity to make their own decisions, to choose their lifestyles and activities, to root for their own baseball teams (as long as they cheer for the Red Sox), to live, to learn, to love, and to believe with freedom and without limits.

The question that frequently shackles me is this: Is the American Dream limited to those from another country? Have resident Americans lost touch with their concept of the American Dream? Have we become complacent? Do we feel, because we were born in the U.S., that the American Dream is our birthright? That it is somehow owed to us? Have we slighted hard work and personal pride for entitlement?

In response to those questions, I've cultivated one more question in my own mind: *Are we, as educators and parents, teaching our children the American Dream?*

We Can Do This!

As educators, we *can* teach—through some direct instruction and intentional role-modeling—what the American Dream means. We can discuss and uncover our own definitions of success. We can determine life choices and educational paths that will lead our students to lives that are better, fuller, richer, greater, happier, more peaceful, enhanced, and funnier. Lives in which they can then make their own, educated, decisions.

- ◆ When a student asks for a gift, a break, or a favor, we can ensure that student works to earn it.
- ◆ When a student argues, we can refuse to engage in an argument, instead providing alternatives for the student to express him- or herself.
- ◆ When a student doesn't work up to his potential, we can insist that he redo the work with more pride.
- ◆ When a student acts in a disrespectful manner toward an adult, we can teach and demand respectful conduct.

- ◆ When a student fails, we can explain the errors and the benefits of correcting them.
- ◆ When a student succeeds, we can illustrate the root of the success and praise the child for a good effort and attitude.
- ◆ When a student needs direction, we can talk about the doors in his or her future and discuss the paths that will lead to them.
- ◆ When appropriate, we can teach the value of a firm handshake, a nice smile, polite manners, and the thought of another person's welfare. And, in case you were wondering, it is *always* appropriate to teach those lessons.
- ◆ Regardless of the socioeconomic circumstance of the child or school, we can teach what Dr. Ruby Payne calls "the hidden rules of middle class"—societal norms that enable students to be successful—for the child to use if he or she so chooses.
- ◆ When a child is in our presence, we can be role models.

America is truly the land of opportunity. Education, especially, opens the many doors of opportunity through which the American Dream lies in wait. As educators, we have all the power in the world to help every child discover his or her own American Dream—in the country where anything is possible.

This year, and every year hence, teaching about the American Dream will be one of my priorities. As a matter of fact, "Reviving the American Dream" is going to be our schoolwide theme and my personal focus until further notice. Won't you join me in reviving it?

600 Reasons to Do It Again Next Year

This essay, originally penned at the conclusion of a school year, contains a message beyond the end-of-the-year blather and melancholy nostalgia. Deep down, whenever we want to, we can turn over a new leaf, turn the page, buy a fresh, new calendar, and start over—ready to rock and roll.

As another school year vanishes in a cloud of dust, sweat, and tears behind us, we're left with time to reflect, to relax (perhaps), and to rejuvenate.

I cannot begin to share the number of times that I've sat alone in my car at the end of a long day of principaling. I sit, unwilling to turn the key as dusk creeps into the staff parking lot, and wonder aloud, "Why, exactly, do I continue to do this?"

As thoughts of testing, budgets, deadlines, lawsuits, conflicts, and the weather cloud my mind, questions rumble louder than my lunch-less belly: Am I really making a difference? Are children truly benefiting from my work? Will the gains we make today expand tomorrow, or will they wither and collapse before the morning bell rings? Am I actually impacting anything in a positive manner?

If you are a human being, you've likely shared some of those same thoughts, or at least some variation of them. You've wondered about your purpose, your goals, your consequences, your influence, your attitude, and your direction. Then, if you're like me, your worries turn toward dinner, picking up the kids, and the rising price of gas. So you hustle home.

When the dust of the day settles and I really have time to reflect, I can always find justification for why I keep at it. Here, from my own experiences, are five of the 600 reasons I saddle up each day—and each year—and ride again.

Jasmin. Jasmin, a delightful yet disheartened student from Mexico, was reading at a pre-primer level midway through fifth grade. About what one would expect from an English-language learner who qualifies for special education, right? That's what the teachers who worked with her thought, and they dropped her from the remedial reading class to get "more bang for their buck" by placing another student with more potential in her spot. That didn't sit well with me, so I assigned the primary-grades reading specialist to work with her. With a little attention, a serving of specific instruction, a dose of encouragement, and some serious love, Jasmin progressed to a mid-second–grade reading level, and her eyes shone again. Although she was still three years below grade level, she now was equipped with confidence, some beginning skills, and the knowledge that she was not alone in this battle.

Manuel. Manuel, another fifth-grade student, was raised in a house where gang activity ruled. To help give him options, we enrolled him in our after-school programs and kept him as occupied as possible in the afternoons. One morning, he was not at school. We soon learned that he was at the hospital with his brother, who had been shot twice during a gang-related squabble. His brother survived, but when Manuel returned to school a few days later he thanked us for steering him straight. He is now our local role model and spokesperson for avoiding gang life. He knows the consequences all too well.

Derek. Derek, who suffers from attention deficit disorder and its associated anxiety and depression, struggled mightily in school throughout his elementary years. During fifth grade, his parents pulled him out of school to live with his grandparents in Montana while they sorted out options for his future. Eventually, they requested a transfer to my school, where they had heard he would get individualized attention and truly differentiated instruction. The change in this young man over the course of his sixth-grade year was staggering. His reading level rose three years to grade level, his self-confidence exploded, and he learned the subtle difference between literal and figurative language. He now understands humor and sarcasm, which opens a million doors for every child.

Becky. At our school, literacy is considered the cornerstone skill of a well-balanced education. Some children, like Becky, have circumstances in their lives that might preclude the necessity to learn to read and write. This seventh-grade student suffers from neurofibromatosis. Her body makes tumors, several of which are inoperable in her brain. Doctors doubt she will celebrate her 15th birthday. Nevertheless, she bounds about campus, smiling from ear to ear as she converses with classmates and teachers, embracing her homework assignments and striving to keep pace with her peers in reading and writing. A few months ago, when her father came to the office to tell us they had purchased their first home and would be leaving our school, he had tears in his eyes as he expressed his gratitude for the development of his daughter. Though she may not have a future, she certainly has a *future*.

Armon. When Armon moved to our town many years ago, he was embarrassed and reluctant to come to school. One of his hands was slightly disfigured, he was academically low, and he teetered on the precipice of gang involvement. Once a week, I drove to his apartment and literally dragged him to school. With the promise of shooting baskets at recess as a hook, he came along. I changed schools and did not see him for five years until the night I attended a high school playoff basketball game. Armon scored 38 points and led his team to victory. When he saw me on the floor after the game, he embraced me warmly and we reminisced about his elementary school days. I kept in touch and watched with pride as he went to college on a full-ride basketball scholarship, and then was drafted into the NBA. When I start to doubt my impact on individual students, I ponder Armon's case: Who knows where he would be if I hadn't put in the relentless effort to keep him in school all those years ago?

When I need a pick-me-up, I turn to my memory bank. I'm sure you can do the same. You can search your own experiences and find those 5, 10, 30, or 600 children who you can use to define your impact. Find the Armons, the Dereks, and the Jasmins of your life, then take a moment to smile. For every Becky, there are 599 others just like her who benefited in subtle, silent ways from your work. For them, you have offered a ray of light, a moment of inspiration, a touch of life—and the only place you'll ever know it is in your own heart. You may never see the ultimate growth, hear the gratitude, read the accomplishments, or observe the changes, but they happen all the same. And you're a big part of it. So saddle up, pardner, and ride again.

REFLECTION QUESTIONS

In Part I, you received a dose of pure, unadulterated liquid motivation. What are you going to do with it? Use the following questions to guide your thinking about the ideas presented in Part I and the strategies you'll employ to implement them to motivate yourself or others. Then make it happen.

1. Consider your professional role. What motivates you? Now consider the people you lead or influence. How are they motivated? What lessons can you learn from the similarities or differences between the two?
2. Do you believe in intrinsic motivation? Do you believe in extrinsic rewards? What circumstances might dictate the application of one form of motivation over the other? How do you know which to choose in any given situation?
3. What does the term "continuous improvement" mean to you? Can you list five examples of how that phrase lives in your work? In your personal life? How can you use those examples to motivate yourself or others?
4. When was the last time you demanded—and by this I mean truly *demanded*—another person's best effort, attention, intensity, or performance? What was it that roused that sense of urgency? What was the result? How can you generate that level of commitment on a regular basis?
5. By contrast, when was the last time you settled for a result far less than you expected, anticipated, or hoped for? Why did you accept mediocrity? Why was "OK" good enough? What can you take from this experience that will help you in a similar situation next time?
6. Review your site goals, your school improvement plan goals, your professional goals, or the goals of someone you lead or influence. Do they meet the SMART definition? Are there specific strategies listed? Will those action steps result in success? If so, congratulate the goal-setter! If not, get to work refining the goals—add intentionality and eliminate "hope."
7. Consider the students with whom you have worked in the past. What lessons have they taught you? Why did those lessons stick with you? What were the circumstances that precipitated that learning? How can you use those lessons

to better keep yourself or others motivated to accomplish what matters most?

8. What are the most important factors in motivating others? Which actions are universal? Which actions are predicated upon the individuals in question? How does your leadership style incorporate these actions?

9. What gets you up in the morning when it's cold, dark, dreary, and you're drained? What is the light that beckons you from yon to keep your engine charged (or to jump-start it when necessary)? Why does that pick-me-up work for you?

PART II

Embrace Change

"Change is inevitable. Progress is optional." John C. Maxwell offered those now-famous words that adorn the walls and stationery of school districts and businesses worldwide. Benjamin Franklin, who predated Mr. Maxwell by some 241 years, had a little more dramatic take on the importance of change: "When you're finished changing, you're finished."

As you'll read in the first essay of Part II, and as you'll hear me repeat over and over again in workshops and ranting monologues during staff meetings and family reunions, "Change is a prerequisite for improvement." If you were paying any attention at all during Part I of the book, you'll know I'm predisposed to position myself and those around me for personal, professional, continuous, and all-encompassing growth. We need change, and we need it to be effective.

As educators, we've come to experience change like a shark experiences the sea: Change is where we live. Sometimes we feel like we're at the surface of it. Other times we can feel it churning. On occasion we ride it out like the tides. And, of course, there are times when we can smell blood in the water and we thrash about madly, frothing our surroundings and sending out waves that ripple well beyond our vision. Change, for better or worse, is the nature of the business.

For teachers, every lesson provides an opportunity for change. Every semester, our class lists change (in elementary school, schools often perform a complete studentectomy over the summer, removing 100 percent of the students in a teacher's class and replacing them with a whole new batch for the upcoming school year), providing incredible new dynamics in the same setting (room 302), in the same course (English 8), with the same instructor (Mrs. Pesky), and the same learning goals, materials, curriculum, textbooks, assignments, assessments, and view out the window.

And then there are the big changes: New administrators arrive, bringing about change. District-level initiatives crop up, changing our focus. Policies and procedures change. Budgets and priorities change. The focus of education in the state legislature, or in the federal government, or in the White House, can change the entire bowl of soup.

Research on how students learn changes our instructional practice. Technology changes faster than a hummingbird's wings flap. Theories on education are updated monthly. Student achievement data illuminate the need to change our perspectives. Organizational flow-charts change the way we do business. As we learn, we grow—and that changes our work. This could go on forever, and it does. How are we supposed to make sense of the changes, adapt to make them successful, and, heavens to Betsy, *lead* the change in our buildings, schools, and districts?

Michael Fullan, a noted expert on educational change, described the behaviors that leaders ought to practice if they are to lead successfully in a high-paced change environment in his 2001 book, *Leading in a Culture of Change*:

> Leaders will increase their effectiveness if they continually work on the five components of leadership—if they pursue moral purpose, understand the change process, develop relationships, foster knowledge building, and strive for coherence—with energy, enthusiasm, and hopefulness. If leaders do so, the rewards and benefits will be enormous. It is an exciting proposition. The culture of change beckons. (p. 11)

Mr. Fullan emphasizes the leadership behaviors that result in positive change. This brings into focus the concept that we haven't fully embraced yet: We *need* change. When things aren't going well, when we're not getting the results we want, when failures abound, when Maxwell's optional "progress" isn't arriving on schedule, and when we need some sort of improvement, we *must* change. It's not just that factors on the outside change our realities, it also rings true that we must change to keep up with the times, to continue to grow, and to improve the outcomes of our work. We must also *seek* change.

Viewed in this light, the idea of change as a desirable phenomenon begs that same question: How do we *lead* the change in our buildings, schools, and districts? Another great organizational leader, Doug Reeves, weighs in (from his 2009 book, *Leading Change in Your School*):

> Failure in change strategies need not be inevitable. In fact, it is avoidable if change leaders will balance their sense of urgency with a more thoughtful approach to implementing change. If we have learned anything about effective change in schools or any complex organization, it is that neither managerial imperatives nor inspirational speeches will be sufficient to move people and organizations from their entrenched positions. (p. 7)

What follows, in Part II of this book, is a collection of essays bound to help leaders accomplish the daunting task of leading change in a comprehensive, intentional, and yes, even inspirational, manner. From discussions of change as an idea (in "Three Steps to Embracing Change"), changing your point of view ("The Power of Positive Phrasing"), or changing what we know ("Get Your Learnin' On"), or how we can accommodate change by taking things off the proverbial plate ("Less Is More"), these discussion starters will empower you and your colleagues to tackle change. This might mean you'll be tackling new challenges, or just tackling challenges anew. It's really up to you. The readings are here to provide the motivation, the inspiration, and a tool or two to help you through it.

Change is the nature of the business, after all.

Three Steps to Embracing Change

Anderson Davis High School is in a world of hurt. The students are not achieving on state assessments, the average daily attendance has dipped below 80 percent, graduation rates are plummeting, violence and graffiti mar the school grounds, and coercing substitutes to spend a day on campus is like trying to teach an ostrich to fly: painful and fruitless.

We've all heard of schools such as Anderson Davis High. Some of us work in schools that match that distasteful description.

For the majority of school administrators, however, schools are happy, positive, and productive places that are good for kids. But are they the idyllic havens for self-actualization, hubs of academic achievement, and breeding grounds of critical thinkers and lifelong learners that we all profess to cultivate? Can we do more for our prized clients, the children themselves? Can we do *better?*

Since that is a rhetorical question, we'll proceed to the *how* part of the conversation. *How* can we improve? *How* can we make our schools the places we would like our own children to attend and where they can flourish? In my research and experience, I have encountered one undeniable fact about school improvement that we, as school leaders, must understand before we can begin to realize the benefits of a true improvement effort: Change is a prerequisite for improvement.

We all know that if we keep doing what we've always done, we'll keep getting what we've always gotten. So why don't we change what we're doing? Because change is difficult, that's why. That is the way we've taught for the past 20 years, and it works. Change is scary, intimidating, disconcerting, and nerve-wracking. It involves stepping out of a comfort zone and into a new realm of reality, one that we call the unknown. And we're all afraid of the unknown. That's why Stephen King's novels sell so well.

So, as leaders of the school improvement movement in our schools, we are faced with the daunting challenge of making change a *necessity,* a *known quantity,* and an *enjoyable prospect.* Yes, you heard me correctly. Let's make change *fun!*

Change Is Necessary

We can use our site achievement data and changing demographic information to graphically demonstrate the *need* to change the way we operate. Pressure from the public, district accountability measures, and Federal programs can help nudge us into a state of understanding that change is necessary. That is not always a pleasant, fun step, but it's crucial. We need to help our staff and school community discover that what we are doing right now is either not working, is not sufficient, or is not sustainable.

If you need more information to help you and your colleagues "confront the brutal facts" of change, I suggest you take a look at Jim Collins' book, *Good to Great.* If we're not honest about what's really happening, we'll never make the necessary adjustments to achieve the gains we're seeking. Conversely, when we peel back the layers and examine the reality of our situations, we'll be much better suited to take the appropriate steps to truly address our needs.

We *Can* Understand the Change Process

There is more research on the stages and process of school improvement available today than ever before. We can dig it out and begin to appreciate what is in store for our schools. We know improvement generally follows a cyclical, self-regulating schedule: define the issues, determine strategies to approach the problems, initiate changes, and evaluate progress and effectiveness ad infinitum. We can share that information with our school communities so they *know* and *understand* the stages, what characteristics each stage exhibits, and how to proceed productively around the cycle. If we continue to revisit these stages while in the throes of the process, we can discern the big picture and understand where we are on the map. Recognizing the steps alleviates the fear and dread that accompany the unawares. It needn't be a mystery.

Change Is Fun

Change is fun. That's right, say it with me: Change is *fun.* That is a secret the auto industry figured out long ago. That's why they invented that "new car smell." It's enjoyable to the olfactory sense but, in actuality, it's merely symbolic of the fact that you have finally traded in the 1985 Toyota Tercel wagon for a 2012 Ford Fusion. We can all upgrade our skills, knowledge, and practices. And what's better than starting a new school year with a new roster of students? Deep down, teachers and everyone else in the school community love change and yearn for a publicly acceptable manner to alter what they do. So let's open the doors for change, celebrate the arrival of new materials, rejoice in new ideas, and revel in new professional discourse.

Personally, I cannot imagine a more apt description of our profession than, "Well, it changes a lot." Change itself is intimately related to our work. It is, in a phrase, the nature of the business. Students enter our doors only to eventually leave—through promotion, graduation, or otherwise moving along. Teachers come and go, administrators switch and are replaced every several years or so, textbooks and curriculum alter with the changing times, neighborhoods transform, technology innovations revolutionize the possibilities within classrooms, and a million *different* experiences assault us every day.

It would almost be foolish to place much stock in the way things were, or even the ways things *are*—because it won't be like that much longer. We're left with only one reality if we're to improve the way we conduct our business: change. As the leaders of our schools, it's our responsibility to recruit the support and backing of the entire school community when embarking upon the school improvement process. And we can get them on board by explaining what change is all about.

A Word of Caution

We might benefit from talking to the teachers from our fictional Anderson Davis High School about the intentionality of change. Changing something just for change's sake can be a powerful leadership strategy, but it can also be a dangerous sword to wield. The folks at Anderson Davis High experienced several leaders and a decade or so of frenetic change—new curriculum, new materials, new expectations, new strategies, but never enough time, emphasis, or support to really master any of them to a degree worthy of sustained, meaningful success.

At Anderson Davis High, it wasn't until a new principal gathered the leadership team and studied the school, the climate, the data, the students, the neighborhood, and the past history of initiatives that the change process yielded fruit.

This team was committed to making informed, intentional decisions—and laying out a plan for making them work over the next three months, year, and three years. It worked, and I guarantee it: They had *fun*!

Get Your Learnin' On

Today there's some good news. Today, the field of education has become stable. The profession has reached its pinnacle. For the first time ever, there is no new information. There are no new research studies. There is no better mousetrap. The methods we use are the Best Practices possible, and there is nothing awaiting us around the next corner. All we need to do, as teachers and school leaders, is to perfect what we already know— and then we never have to learn to do anything new or differently.

Wake up! You're dreaming!

Education fluctuates more than a rattlesnake's temperature. Maybe it's a pendulum. Perhaps it's a cycle. It could be a spiral. Possibly it's an atomic explosion. Who knows? The point is this: With all the resources at our disposal, and the information at our fingertips, all the data clamoring to capture our attention, all the advancements in learning, and all the research supporting new and innovative strategies, this business of education changes daily. *Daily*, I tell you.

We can always do better today than we did yesterday, and we can invariably do better than that tomorrow. In order to stay abreast of the latest and greatest teaching methods, school structures, innovative strategies, comprehensive programs, detailed research, and curriculum materials, we need to avoid resting on our laurels. We cannot wait for two years, heads buried in the sand, then emerge and ask, "What did I miss? What do I need to do to catch up?" Education moves much too fast for that.

A Proactive Approach

What can we do to keep our heads in the game? How can we ensure that our learning is running parallel to the profession itself? Where can we look for the information we need to lead our schools well into the 21st Century? Well, loyal readers, reading this essay and bookmarking www.educationworld .com is a good start, so you're to be commended . . . and here are some other ideas:

Join a professional organization—or three. Are you a member of the Association for Supervision and Curriculum Development (ASCD)? How about the National Association of Elementary School Principals (NAESP) or the National Association of Secondary School Principals (NASSP)? Have you joined Phi Delta Kappa? The International Reading Association (IRA)? National Council of Teachers of Mathematics (NCTM)? National Council for the Social Studies (NCSS)? The list is endless, and each of these professional organizations offers up-to-date research and articles in their journals, as well as a plethora of other resources: CDs, books, regional and national conferences, guides, blogs, newsletters, and more.

Read, read, read. In addition to the journals published by the resources above, there is a variety of materials out there just yearning to be picked up and read. Education Week is the nation's education newspaper and provides articles ranging from worldwide education to the candidates' positions on schooling and everything in between. Don't have time to go through all the journals and magazines? No worries. Kim Marshall, a lifelong educator, summarizes the key articles from 44 journals in his Marshall Memo; he takes the guesswork out of our professional reading.

Grab a book. There are a lot of good books on education out there. Yes, it's difficult to tell who is a credible author and which methods will yield positive results for your work in your school, but that's the beauty of thinking while you're reading. Take the cap off the highlighter, open the book, and start critically reading. If you have trouble dedicating the time to such professional reading, recruit the involvement of colleagues and use their peer pressure. Start a book club—read the text, discuss it together, and create some action plans to make use of your new learning. Between professional books, you'll still have time for Stephen King and whoever just climbed onto Oprah's book list.

Sit in on your teachers' collaborative meetings. We already do this for accountability, to provide the resources at our disposal, and to help analyze data, but how often do we sit down with our best and brightest teachers just to learn? It's amazing what our people know. Listen to them. Crash a grade level's team meeting and point your ears inward. Invite your specialists to breakfast and listen to them banter. Ask your experts to attack a challenging curriculum problem, sit back, have some popcorn, and take notes. Don't have any superstars? Get a second opinion—every school does.

Attend a conference. Ah, yes, the highly attractive opportunity to spend more time in meetings. If you haven't been to a national, regional, or even local conference, you're in for a treat. These days, our profession has some phenomenal presenters leading workshops, learning sessions, discussions, and other presentations designed to inform, confront, inspire, challenge, reinforce, motivate, and/or rouse the natural yearning for learning you already possess. The information is limitless, so the key is to attend a conference that meets some very specific needs for you and your organization—not just one that's located in an exotic locale, like Bermuda. Chart out your course, determine which speakers and which topics are of greatest interest to you, and start filling up your tool belt.

Teach a class. The sky's the limit here. This could mean you take over a kindergarten for an hour and teach them the concept of subtraction, or it could mean you lead a whole-staff professional development session on the use of formative assessments. Perhaps you interpret this as guest lecturing at the local college in a beginning teachers' class, or leading a session at a regional education conference. Research tells us we retain 10–15 percent of what we hear in a workshop, but 90 percent sticks with us if we teach it to someone else. Go take this on, especially in an area you might not consider yourself an expert in. The learning curve is steep, but worth the climb.

Sure, some of the items in this list cost money. So does breakfast, but you don't skip the most important meal of the day, do you? Eschewing your own learning is a health crime against your professional well-being, and we, as educational leaders, have the responsibility to know what's going on in the world of education. Then, and only then, can we make strides to lead the growth and progress our schools deserve. What steps are you willing to take to ensure that you're ahead of the game, or at least on the same playing field as everyone else?

Two Pieces of the High-Quality Puzzle

There's an indelible truth out there in our schools, academies, and educational institutions nowadays: Schools matter. Teaching makes a difference. Effective teaching saves lives. Just in case I'm not preaching to the choir, allow me to share a couple of quotes that might reinforce this point:

- ◆ "The one factor that can make the most difference in improving student achievement is a knowledgeable, skillful teacher in front of the classroom." (National Commission on Teaching and America's Future, 1996)
- ◆ "Success in education hinges on what happens at the classroom level." (Thomas Guskey, 2002)
- ◆ "Improved classroom instruction is the prime factor to produce student achievement gains." (Odden & Wallace, 2003)
- ◆ "One can conclude that the question as to whether effective teachers make a significant difference in student achievement has been answered. They do!" (Robert Marzano, 2007)
- ◆ "Those who educate children well are more to be honored than they who produce them; for these only gave them life, those the art of living well." (Aristotle, circa 325 B.C.)

Aristotle's quote is included just to demonstrate that the reverence for educators is a stance long held by polite society, not some newfangled idea some author made up. I could go on and on with the quotes, the citations, the references, and the evidence, but instead I'll give you two options: 1) Believe that high-quality teaching can truly make a difference in children's lives and keep reading, or 2) Doubt that teachers can influence anything and go back to lawn bowling. Of course, poor teaching can also influence children, as hilarious actor Woody Allen realized: "I had a terrible education. I attended a school for emotionally disturbed teachers." That might start the chicken-or-the-egg debate, but that's not really what we're here to analyze right now.

Quality Teaching: What Is It?

Make no mistake, teaching moves matter. The ability to engage students, the selection of instructional techniques, the creation of deep learning experiences, the utilization of formative assessment tools, and the establishment of classroom rules and procedures all play a role in answering the question, "What does an effective teacher do?" However, I'll boil it down to its most basic, root elements. Down to the atomic level, or further: even beyond the nucleus. What follows are the two most central characteristics of successful teachers. To narrow it down any further, you'd need a particle accelerator and a boatload of superconducting magnets.

Intentionality

Few individual instructional strategies would trump the idea that the most effective strategies are the ones chosen and delivered *on purpose*. Sure, the lists of "Best Practices" devised as a result of research-based analysis of teaching methods, such as Marzano's "Classroom Instruction That Works" (2001) and Hattie's "Visible Learning" (2009), provide us with a wealth of effective pedagogical approaches, but they don't result in better student learning outcomes simply because they exist, do they? No. These are proven to be effective strategies because teachers selected them intentionally from all the choices at their disposal.

Successful teachers choose their weapons on purpose, as part of a plan to maximize learning. Is it any wonder that the very first domain in Charlotte Danielson's indispensable *Framework for Teaching* is entitled "Planning and Preparation"?

Think about the most effective teachers you've worked alongside, observed, supervised, or had the pleasure of learning from. How much of that teacher's lesson construct, delivery, discussion, and assessment were based in happenstance? Probably little less than a surgeon's arthroscopic procedure to repair your uncle's torn anterior cruciate ligament. Successes just aren't realized from the seats of our pants.

Before any lessons are learned, the high-quality teacher identifies the clear learning objective, considers the students, and then creates and designs a plan to assist the students in achieving mastery of that objective. Good teaching isn't random, it rarely proceeds from page one to page 323 in linear order, and it's much different than "playing school" in your friend Emily's basement when you were a kid. Our top-notch teachers recognize this necessity for forethought, embrace it, and make it part of the regular routine. And they ensure that everything they do and say during a lesson—everything—is done and said for a reason.

Self-Reflection

John Dewey said it best: "It's not the doing that matters. It's the thinking about the doing." In the last century or so since Dewey's research on the way we think and its relationship to our deeds and progress, organizations in all arenas have recognized the impact of individuals' reflective behaviors. Nowhere is this more prominent than in the fourth Core Proposition that steadies the National Board of Professional Teaching Standards (NBPTS): "Teachers think systematically about their practice and learn from experience."

The NBPTS, acknowledged as America's loftiest status achievement for educators, prizes the practice of self-reflection, adding, "Striving to strengthen their teaching, accomplished teachers examine their practice critically; expand their repertoire; deepen their knowledge; sharpen their judgment; and adapt their teaching to new findings, ideas, and theories."

A few years ago, I worked with a colleague to unearth as much research on the benefits of self-reflection as our flashdrives would hold. In our book, "Building Teachers' Capacity for Success," Alisa Simeral and I identified four stages that teachers progress through as they increase their ability to accurately and consistently reflect upon the results of their teaching decisions. Those stages are: Unaware, Conscious, Action, and Refinement.

The goal for us, as instructional leaders, is to usher our teachers toward the Refinement stage, at which educators polish their reflective tendencies before, during, and after lessons. They select strategies based upon student need, learning styles, past history, and dozens of other factors. They've selected a course of action *intentionally*, but they're also willing and able to adapt said lesson on the fly, *should the situation dictate charting a new course of action*. For Refinement stage teachers, lesson delivery and student mastery truly comprise an art form, one parallel to Claude Monet, Michelangelo, Fabergé, Pablo Picasso, or Guy Ritchie.

Are These Characteristics Universal?

The question is truly this: Can any teacher be intentional and self-reflective? The answer is a resounding and unambiguous yes. The dispositions, however, must be emphasized and reinforced as a priority even more than the actions themselves.

School leaders can and must decisively insist that teachers create and follow well thought out, articulated plans for addressing students' needs and meeting overtly communicated learning goals. There will be no winging it in our schools, folks, not if we're truly about student learning.

School leaders can and must provide ample opportunity for teachers to engage in critical self-reflection, offering targeted feedback and sharing reflective prompts that generate thought, introspection, discussion, and debate. There will be no, "I taught it. What's next?" in our schools, folks, not if we're truly about student learning.

Intentionality and Self-Reflection: With these two teaching behaviors solidly stationed at the foundation of our regular routines, the rest are just details. If we can lead our legions of educators to emphasize these two traits, we can empower them to master the instructional universe. When our teachers engage in these actions, we can successfully avoid the scenario comedian George Burns found himself in: "Smartness runs in my family. When I was in school I was so smart my teacher was in my class for five years."

Less Is More

We've got district initiatives, government regulations, grant stipulations, contracted obligations, state mandate, and the list goes on. Our plates are full! Let's remove some of the clutter from our plates by removing some of the clutter from our teachers' plates.

Spotted on the grounds of the Old Penitentiary in Boise, Idaho, a modest tombstone bears the following carved inscription:

> Here lies the body of Lester Moore
> Shot by a guard with a .44
> Now there is no Les no more

Today we're going to present the argument that less (Les) is indeed more (Moore), at least in schools. We'll leave the argument for prisons to sociologists and political activists, though it was early education reformer Horace Mann who noted, "Jails and prisons are the complement of schools; so many less as you have of the latter, so many more must you have of the former."

Education Today

Think about today's schools. We've got district initiatives, government regulations, grant stipulations, contracted obligations, state mandates, and more. There are a million different pushes coming from as many different directions. Meanwhile, as our research about how our brains work becomes more sophisticated, and as we gather more and better information about how children learn, the deluge of directions about how we ought to teach comes pouring down upon us.

So what do we, as responsible principals acting as the buffer, do to our staffs? We bury them in committees, schedules, supervision, volunteer programs, data analysis, before- and after-school meetings, materials, activities and evening events, training, and special programs. Sprinkle a little goal-setting, demands, testing, accountability, evaluations, and relentlessly high expectations for change and improvement on top for good measure. But we have to realize this: their plates are full. Heck, *our* plates are full too. We need a buffer—a steel umbrella, actually!

Let's remove some of the clutter from our plates by removing some of the clutter from their plates. Instead of trying to do everything perfectly and right now, let's allocate our energies into doing the most important items well. After all, these are the most essential and necessary pieces of our instructional puzzles.

Simplicity

In minimalist architecture, building designs emphasize the necessary elements and eschew the extraneous, which magnifies the natural aesthetics and increases practicality. In schools, we don't have to be Álvaro Siza Vieira to design an education system that works more economically. We don't need fancy programs, the newest doohickeys, outlandish materials, and matching laptops to teach children to read, to perform scientific investigations, and to uncover the relationship between hard work and success.

We need instead to KISS (Keep It Simple, Stupid) and focus on:

Relationships. Programs don't teach children, teachers teach children. Think back to your own school days for a moment. Which was the teacher you might consider the best one you ever had? Probably not the one with the most content knowledge, likely not the one with the coolest wardrobe, surely not the one with the most elaborate materials, and definitely not the one who followed an instructional program lock-step like a droid. If you're like every other adult I've met, yours was that special teacher who got to know you the best, the teacher who spent time making you feel worthwhile. The teacher made you feel like you had potential and believed in you. That relationship piece that we take for granted too often—that we ignore because of curriculum and pacing demands, and that we shrug off when discussing our toughest kids—is the piece that separates the great teacher from the ordinary. It may well make the difference between a child's success and failure.

Goal-setting. Did you ever think that Stephen Covey may have been on to something when he penned chapter two, "Begin with the end in mind," from his landmark book *The 7 Habits of Highly Effective People*? How much precious time and valuable energy have we frittered away chasing our highly-educated tails? Have you ever observed a teacher droning through a lesson from a textbook just because it was the next lesson in the textbook, even though it might not match the grade-level standards or the essential learning outcomes for the course? Remember (yesterday) when you winced while watching a teacher meander aimlessly through a lesson, leading the students in an activity, or passing time with a discussion that went absolutely and indefatigably nowhere at all? When we set goals and identify a target, we can chart a path that will lead us to our intended destination without the detours or tangential distractions.

Prioritization. True prioritization, as I've quoted Mr. Covey before, comes from identifying the most urgent and important behaviors, and acting upon them. Here's where the steel umbrella buffer comes into play: We need to shield our staffs from the barrage of initiatives and pushes so they can focus on the most essential elements of their professional duties. What's the most important thing? Maybe it's building relationships. Perhaps it's streamlining the curriculum. Possibly it's creating thorough end-of-unit assessments. It could be identifying the learning objectives for each unit of study. When we can focus on something—anything—we can learn more about it, we can experience it with more depth and precision, and we can maximize our efforts. This is a step we must take if we're to truly live in accordance with our mission, for it is that which drives us to do anything and everything. If not, we ought to say no.

Elimination. Any good pediatrician will explain the importance of practicing healthy elimination routines, and we'll follow their lead by encouraging educators to get rid of the excess. Here's a good ratio:

For every new directive or adoption, we should select two nonessential activities to remove. There is always a newer and better mousetrap coming down the pike, and when it arrives it should replace the old one and the outdated snares that accompany it. Without a solid process of elimination, we find ourselves backed up and spread so thinly that we can't really accomplish anything with any degree of effectiveness. Success will escape us. Don't believe it? Let's get healthy. Try tackling a new diet. Then tack on a new exercise regimen. Now enroll in a yoga class. Try adding acupuncture. You read about a highly effective new diet, so you'd better try that, too. Are you taking stress medication? If not, you'd better start. You're not getting healthier. Instead, you're overwhelming yourself to the point of no return. Pretty soon you'll be passed out on the couch next to an empty pint of Häagen-Dazs with pins in your eyeballs and one leg stuck helplessly behind your head.

We can create for ourselves a better, happier, balanced, focused future. It's up to us. What will it read on your tombstone?

The Power of Positive Phrasing

When my daughter was born, it was 4:06 in the afternoon. That's a magical number for baseball fans: Legendary Red Sox outfielder Ted Williams batted .406 in 1941, and no batter has topped .400 since. In military time, 4:06 p.m. is actually 1606 hours, and when a certain mathematical savant author adds the digits 1+6+0+6 he gets 13, which many consider to be a lucky number. Of course, I also invite black cats to cross my path as I walk under ladders. (Popular superstitions don't bother me.) The point is the kid rocketed off to a good start.

Anyhow, my daughter's a gymnast. During her second season of competitive gym, her balance beam routine included a cartwheel. For those of us who cannot execute a cartwheel on a basketball court with spotters, the prospect of flipping upside-down on a six-inch-wide beam four feet above the ground makes our feet sweat, our pulses race, and our knees buckle. However, this is a maneuver my daughter had completed in practices, so there it was in her routine.

Five meets that season, five cartwheels on the beam, and five falls later, my distraught offspring and I shared a conversation after dinner at IHOP, and we determined that the falls were no longer physical. They were constructs of her mind. She had talked herself into falling because prior to every meet she had told herself, "Don't fall off the beam."

Just as we might focus on the word "worry" when someone says "Don't worry," or on the words "stressed out" when a well-meaning friend implores "Don't be stressed out," my daughter's focus was on the "fall off," not the "don't."

We'll get into the details of how the brain ignores the "don't" part of that request in a minute, but for now suffice it to say she was focused on the wrong part of her routine. She needed to focus on sticking the landing on her cartwheel.

In the final meet of the season—the State championships, no less—she nailed that cartwheel like she was on the gym floor with spotters. No fear. No hesitation. Not even a wobble of the knees!

In our post-meet embrace, she told me this: "Dad, for the past two weeks, since that last meet, I've been telling myself, '*Stick* the cartwheel, *stick* the cartwheel.' And I did."

Lessons for Educators

We educators can learn something from this. As much as I am thrilled that my daughter stuck her cartwheel, I'm even more convinced that the idea of positive phrasing works. On a variety of different levels, we experience more success and harvest more positive results when we harness the power of our words.

To support that idea in school leadership, please welcome Mrs. Galen Hoffstadt, a National Distinguished Principal from Corpus Christi, Texas. Galen is perhaps one of the most positive, motivational, inspirational individuals I've had the good fortune to meet, and she's a staunch advocate of positive phrasing. Everything she says has a positive twist to it, and one can't help but smile and think optimistically when in her presence.

Success Is Within Your Reach and Your Mind

As a school leader, Galen must rally her troops toward a vision of the future—in a positive way. When asked about her students in the year 2019, for example, she might say "Our scholars thirst for knowledge, see from different perspectives, and bring their necessary tools."

Since our unconscious brain filters out words like "don't," "no," and "not," Galen is wise to avoid saying "Our scholars don't get lazy, aren't self-absorbed, and do not arrive unprepared."

See, there's a big difference in the way we phrase things, even though the intended meaning may be identical.

Think of all the times we've engaged in a conversation with a teacher, a student, a parent, a superintendent, or a local business leader. The images we portray, the energy we emit, the confidence we exude, and the responses we elicit are predicated entirely upon the way we present ourselves, in particular, through our words.

Here are a couple of simple ways we can ensure that our words are uplifting and inspiring:

Use positive words. Words matter. Words are powerful. Words can lift, or words can destroy. Let's use the power of our words for good, not for evil. We tend to get more of what we focus on—so let's focus on what we want to happen. The next time you're chatting with another school person, reflect upon the objective of your conversation. Then, realign your thoughts and spoken words on that intended outcome. One of your teachers, Mrs. Howard, says she wants her student, Mikayla, to stop blurting out and disrupting the class discussions. You can help Mrs. Howard realize that what she really wants is for Mikayla to speak at appropriate times and respect the classroom discourse. This can steer a conversation away from punishment and frustration—and nudge us toward teaching and guidance, which are, after all, two of the pillars upon which we've staked our professional claim.

Don't say don't. Never say never. We learned this in teaching school: When we create classroom rules, we want to avoid telling students what *not* to do. Rather, we'd like to provide them with clear expectations of what *to* do. Try this:

Don't think of a ring-tailed lemur.

Goodness, you just got an image in your head of a ring-tailed lemur, didn't you? Even though I told you not to. Imagine what a naughty essay-reader you are!

Now try this:

Think of an erupting volcano.

Great, you did it!

Imagine the possibilities if we told students "Please walk," instead of "Don't run," if we asked our teachers to, "Please make every effort to engage your students in your lessons" instead of, "Don't just lecture and hand out worksheets," if we asked our parents "Remember to attend parent-teacher conferences next week" instead of "Don't forget next week is conference week," and if we implored ourselves to, "Prepare thoroughly for every staff meeting" instead of, "Never come to a meeting unprepared."

If it'll help, keep tally-marks on how many times you advise folks *not* to do something—with the best of interests, of course—over the course of a week. Then turn it around.

Embrace optimism. When you find yourself staring at a glass, focus your energy on the half that is full. Henry Ford once said, "Whether you think you can or whether you think you can't, you're right." Every situation presented to us affords us the chance to choose. Our choice can be to proceed with optimism, believing we're on a winning streak and we can overcome any obstacle in our path, or to continue pessimistically, pointing out all the pitfalls and potential failures that might befall us. Odds are, the choice we make will be the reality that follows. Some call this a self-fulfilling prophecy; I don't believe in prophecies, so I'll submit that I believe it is reality. We determine our own fate, we control our destiny, and we influence our own reality—so let's emphasize the limitless possibilities within ourselves, aim for the stars, and give a big bear hug to that beautiful entity called Opportunity.

Then, let's hop onto a six-inch-wide beam, four feet above the ground, and start cartwheeling. Just make sure you stick it.

Morphing Your School into a *Literacy Academy*

Our progress as a nation can be no swifter than our progress in education. Our requirements for world leadership, our hopes for economic growth, and the demands of citizenship itself in an era such as this all require the maximum development of every young American's capacity. The human mind is our fundamental resource.

Times have changed since President John F. Kennedy delivered that *Special Message to the Congress on Education* on February 20, 1961.

Or have they?

Are we in any less dire circumstances in the global economy? Is our position in international relations any less strained? Is our preeminence in worldwide competition any less threatened? Is our need to fully educate every child any less vital to our existence and prosperity?

The purposes and values of education are many and varied. If you read the mission and vision statements of the tens of thousands of U.S. schools, you will see an interesting blend of purposes and ambitions, playing out in an even wider array of philosophies and mindsets.

Of all the skills we teach our students, of all the lessons we lead, of all the activities we facilitate, of all the barriers we traverse, of all the goals we chase, of all the abilities we endorse, the single most crucial, critical, elemental, important, indispensable, and worthwhile is literacy. The ability to read, write, and communicate is second to none.

Think about how often we use those abilities. (In fact, what are you doing right now?) On a daily basis we read newspapers, books, magazines, journals, articles, online chat rooms, diaries, movie credits, phone books, TV guides, fliers, advertisements, menus, recipes, street signs, billboards, graffiti, shopping lists, and a million other things. And somebody had to write them.

Many cultures pass along tales and traditions from generation to generation. Ours is a literature-based society. History books, etchings on walls, remnants of papyrus scrolls, chiseled stone tablets, and CD labels define and chronicle our past and future. It is the literacy skills that survive us and allow this transmission of information.

How does this relate to education in the Era of Accountability? In this era, like in Kennedy's, education is of paramount importance. And the education that we provide our children ought to remain staunchly focused on the most fundamental, important skills: literacy.

A New Definition of Schools

What I propose is a new definition of our schools, especially the ones that have students in them "whose schooling is of interest to us," to quote Ron Edmonds of Harvard (1978). Why not shift the mindset a bit and call them what they really need to be—*literacy academies?*

If we are to prepare our students for their citizenship in society, and if we can offer them the foundation of a solid education, and if we can assure them the building-block skills that will allow them the liberties to explore a wide variety of content and information as they grow in years: Why not dedicate the crucial first few years of schooling to the teaching and learning of literacy skills, above all else? Then, to round out the experience all the way through high school, let's keep bolstering those skills until graduation day. Any school can do it. There are model schools that excel in literacy education splattered across the United States, and we can learn from them. What follows is a summary of the key components that combine to provide the structure for turning a garden-variety neighborhood school into a hub of literacy.

Define your outcomes. As a school community, the first step is rational enough: Identify your mission, vision, and goals. Why is a literacy academy an attractive solution for education in today's world? When you have achieved full *literacy academy* status, what will that look like? What skills will your students possess? What preparation and knowledge will they have acquired? How are they better suited to face the big, bad world as a result of their educational experiences? Beyond the hype and the curricular clutter we currently wade through, our young people need to be able to read, write, and communicate. You'll find these skills peppered throughout the Common Core Standards for a reason: This is a good start, and it's the foundation upon which everything else can be learned.

Focus your professional development. In his book *Good to Great*, Jim Collins refers to a clear concept that guides all of one's efforts, which he calls the "hedgehog concept." Once you have identified your hedgehog concept, you can begin the work of aligning your staff's professional development with it. Bringing in trainers, offering stipends for literacy-focused action research projects, sending staff to conferences and workshops, encouraging teachers to model and observe each other, offering book clubs, engaging in instructional coaching, or one of a plethora of professional development options can support the school's mission and vision. The improvement of literacy instruction, with the ultimate goal of increasing literacy achievement, depends on the development of the teachers. They are only as good as they know how to be.

Teach content through literacy. We would be remiss to bypass the important content areas of science, social studies, mathematics, the arts, physical education, and, as a personal plug, baseball history. Each of those subject areas has its place in the education of every child, and each, not surprisingly, can be taught through literacy. Success in integrating content into literacy instruction is not contingent upon having a ton of reading materials at every child's individual level for every topic; rather, it involves utilizing solid literacy-focused instructional strategies to teach the content areas. A serious dedication and laser-like focus on literacy-based instructional methods does not preclude a well-rounded education. In fact, it is a requirement of one.

Establish a framework of support and resources. An endeavor as complicated and intricate as this demands all the support and scaffolds you can provide. Challenging the status quo and shifting a major instructional paradigm is not the type of venture one should embark upon solo. Groups of teachers facing similar struggles, equipped with similar skills and confronting similar needs, can make remarkable gains when they put their heads together. When we establish the team-first approach to problem solving, the avenues of learning and growth open up, lending squadrons of educators to work, plan, train, assist, brainstorm, assess, and analyze together toward a common end. Couple the "musketeer" approach with resources—both financial and time—aligned to the hedgehog concept, and you have the makings of a true success story.

Share the joy of literacy learning with the entire school community. Have fun with reading, writing, and communicating! For heaven's sake, these are children we're trying to educate, and what do children do better than have fun? Children, not unlike adults and kittens, learn better, perform better, attend better, and live better when they are enjoying the activities in which they are engaged. School should be fun, and a literacy-based instructional approach should be no different. Writing contests, reading challenges, utilizing a variety of reading sources, investigating a variety of genres, recruiting students' input in content areas, word games, literacy-based assemblies, and any of about a billion other activities can spruce up the instruction, rev up the motivation, and amp up the student body. We have no greater calling.

Changing Addresses

Originally written in the spring of a year in which the domino effect of principals swapping offices was particularly overwhelming, this essay is worth forwarding to any principal you know who will have a new position in the coming school year. This could include brand-new principals receiving their first assignment or veteran principals moving to a new school or district . . .

Around this time of year, school districts nationwide are deep into the planning process for the upcoming school year. That's because they've already confirmed the end-of-the-year administrator party and decided which hors d'oeuvres to serve, so there's nothing more pressing to do just now.

And if your district is anything like Generic District 44 in suburban Metropolis, it's putting the finishing touches on its administrator assignments for the coming school year. More than likely, there will be a few new principals (or some principals assigned to different schools) in the mix—and this essay is for them.

Congratulations, You're a Principal

If you are a new principal, *congratulations!* I hope someone bought you a five-gallon tub of antibacterial hand sanitizer and a seat belt. This is a dirty job, so buckle up! However, this is also a great job. I say that the principalship is the single most influential position in education today.

If you're a principal moving to a different school, *congratulations!* We all need a fresh start every once in a while. No matter what your past experiences have been, a change of locale brings a plethora of new opportunities. This is a new chance to make a significant impact in the lives of hundreds, maybe thousands, of young people.

Ever since your new appointment, you've probably heard a lot of advice, some of which may include this gem: *Enter slowly. Don't make any changes that first year.* Well, that's hogwash! You were hired to be the principal of that school for a reason, and if that reason in any way resembles, "Improve student achievement, staff morale, teacher quality, cost effectiveness, parent involvement, traffic flow, and schoolwide discipline," then you'd better make some changes. Remember, change is a prerequisite of improvement.

So use your skills, knowledge, and resources to discover the changes you need to make, and make them. You're the principal, right? I already congratulated you. You don't hibernate during Year One and suddenly awaken as an Action Principal at the onset of Year Two, so be the principal starting now.

Practical Advice

Instead of the nonsensical "Take a ten-month nap" advice you may have received, I've compiled a simple list of three things you can do to help make a positive transition in your new position:

1. Meet with every single employee of the school. *(Warning: Metaphor approaching!)* Pick up a rock and throw it. Forget two birds, because this activity could possibly take out the whole flock! Here is your opportunity to:

- ◆ Get to know the staff members you'll be working with for the next few years.
- ◆ Find out what some of the staff members' big concerns are.
- ◆ Set some foundational work for your nonnegotiables and your vision.
- ◆ Demonstrate that individual voices matter to you and that you are approachable.

- ◆ Gather crucial information that will help you make some initial decisions.
- ◆ Begin to build relationships with personnel.
- ◆ Establish yourself as the authority figure.
- ◆ Become familiar with the faces of your staff so that first back-to-school staff meeting is more like "The Partridge Family" rather than "The Addams Family."

That's a tall order, you say? How will you ever have time to do that? Start now, if you're within striking distance of the new school. Make yourself available before and after school. Put a schedule on the office counter so the staff can sign up. If you can't do that now (for example, if you live more than 30 miles from the new school, or if a meteor strikes your automobile), set aside open-office time during the summer. If you don't take the time now, it'll take you three to four times as long to accomplish the short list of benefits above. The point is this: Make yourself available.

And always remember this: You have one mouth and two ears, so talk some, but listen a lot.

2. Take everything out of the office. Everything. Then start over. (Wait for the outgoing principal to vacate the office before you take this step, otherwise it's horrendously bad advice.) This step is as metaphorical as it is practical. The ex-principal had a certain way of doing things, and you have a certain way of doing things. Chances are they are different ways, which is healthy and perfectly fine for everyone. Once we accept that reality, we can begin to act on it.

When I say take everything out of the office, I do mean *everything*. Desk, file cabinets, tables, chairs, binders, cobwebs, posters, boxes, plants, bobblehead dolls, fire extinguishers—everything. And when I say start over, I do mean *start over*. From scratch! Begin with cleaning. Scour it, scrub it down, wipe off the walls and doorknobs, paint what needs to be painted, and clean the windows. If the windows can't be cleaned because of scratches or because they're cheap plexiglass, break them and have them replaced. This is a principal's office, not a dungeon.

Once it's clean, and you've persuaded the superintendent that the windows really were broken from an errant soccer ball kicked from *outside* the office, then you can refill that space the way *you* will use it best. After you've got your furniture and major items inside (empty file cabinets strategically placed, computer smartly located, and a clear path from your desk to an emergency exit—you never know when an angry parent or over-eager software salesman is going to come storming in), then you can start the tedious process of going through the piles of—how do you say this in English?—*junk* that is now piled thigh-deep in the main office.

Here's an idea: File it in the dumpster. Most of it will never be missed, and those truly essential binders are replaceable. If they're that important, there can't just be one in the entire district, can there? On second thought, you probably ought to go through the piles of, um, *stuff* more carefully than that so you can partially refill those file cabinets, but the point is simple: Only place what *you* know *you* will need back into that office. It's yours, you know.

3. Walk the neighborhood. Go for a walk around the school. Get a lay of the land. Don't be shy about taking a map with you so you can examine your zoning boundaries because you learn a tremendous amount when you obtain a feel for where your students are coming from. Introduce yourself to the folks you meet on the street, paying special attention to being cordial— and avoiding broken glass because first impressions matter, and you don't need an infection.

Visit the stores and restaurants in your school zone. Maybe even pick up some gift certificates to use as rewards for staff or as birthday presents for your in-laws. It's nice to support the local merchants, and it sets a positive tone for your relationships with those business owners. Perhaps some day in the near future you'll be back around looking to create some partnerships between the school and community. You've already built a strong foundation.

Take this walk a couple of times, hitting different side streets and focusing on tough intersections children might have to cross to get to school. Are there parks in the neighborhood? Are children playing there? Is there graffiti painted on buildings? Is it legible? Spelled correctly? Pick up every bit of information you can. You will probably meet more than a few of your future

(I mean *current*) students, and they can give you all sorts of information as well. Plus you'll get some fresh air and put some steps on your pedometer. Again, two (or more) birds with one stone!

Congratulations!

Did I already congratulate you? Yes, that was on your assignment. Now I'm offering my congratulations on taking three rather simple steps that can be critically important to your transition as the new principal of Wonderschool. I'm sure you'll be a hit at your new address. Go get 'em!

My Three Favorite Things: Data, Data, and Data

Educators, as a breed, are afraid of data. We shy away from them, shun them, and generally treat them like contagious numerical pathogens. After all, for decades—centuries, even— we have been the evaluators, assigning grades and pointing out errors our students make. But now we are on the other side of the evaluation, often left to the mercy of unpleasant school designations and ugly press descriptions.

But those fears and mistrust are misguided. Earl and Katz (2006), in *Leading Schools in a Data-Rich World*, state flatly, "Data, by themselves, are benign. Meaning is brought to data by the human act of interpretation." So what we really fear and mistrust are politicians and newspaper reporters. Some big revelation.

Data are wonderful, and in the right hands they can help school officials and teachers make tremendous decisions to support the learning goals of their students. And, last I checked, that was still one of the major tenets of the American public school system.

Definitions We Need to Know

Data are bits of information, nothing more. Remember, they are benign. They indicate the number of items correct, percent of students scoring 75 or higher, number of minutes spent teaching math, words correct per minute, or measure of the angle of a sharpened pencil. Data points are simply pieces of information, facts awaiting analysis, evidence of learning anticipating scrutiny, details pending examination. They sit there, in rows and columns, on spreadsheets or notepads, patient and passive while we determine their purpose.

Formative data are bits of information that we use to guide future decision-making. In the real world, they are the results of a medical exam from which a doctor can determine the cause of abdominal pain and prescribe a course of treatment. In a school setting, they are the results of an introductory literacy assessment from which a teacher can plan instruction to help the student improve reading comprehension strategies.

Summative data are pieces of information that we use to perform a final analysis. They are the equivalent of an autopsy, which is an all too familiar metaphor to principals of schools designated as "failing" by a certain Federal accountability program (No Child Left Behind). Summative data give us final grades and tell us how much in taxes we owe. By the time they show up on the scene, it's too late to do anything about them.

So Why Do I Like Data?

Data provide us with feedback and guidance. They awaken us to our successes and failures, sharing information that allows us to alter our paths or to forge forth, depending on the scenario. But in order for the data to be truly useful, we need to remember one fundamental law of data existence: We are in charge of the data, not vice versa.

We should repel data that arrive on our doorstep unannounced and uninvited. They are pretentious little bits of information that know not their own boundaries. We should also buck data that land upon our laps out of thin air. They are no more than overstepping parasites wishing to feed upon our decaying academic flesh.

No, for data to be beneficial, they should agree with their fate and wait for us to engage in "the human act of interpretation." We should hunt them down in a giant numerical and informational big-game safari. We should identify, track, and hone in on specific bits of information that we need to answer questions we have, then target those data in our scopes and fire away.

Here are the questions we need to answer in order to acquire the data we need so that we can all share a love of data.

What data do we need? What are we trying to determine? What do we want to know? Do we need formative data or summative data? Are we evaluating the implementation of a new program? Are we examining career and college readiness programs for our ninth graders? Are we preparing to design instruction for a third grade science unit? Or are we crafting interventions for students struggling with reading fluency? Only when we know what we need the data for should we even begin identifying them.

What data will answer these questions? What information works to support these needs? Will assessment scores provide accurate data, or do we need more objective information? Would a combination of assessments provide well-rounded data sources that address the issues at hand? Do we even have the tools that return such information, or should we continue to seek the data sources that can fulfill the task? After we have found the proper data sources, we can begin to collect the bits of information we need to proceed.

Did we collect enough data? Are there bits of information missing that are essential to fully answering the questions that began this quest? Are the data reliable (duplicable) and valid (accurate)? If necessary, retrace the steps and obtain more or critical pieces that complete the puzzle. Then, we can hire the data into their ultimate employment as we take the next step: data analysis.

What do the data tell us? When we put the data to the test, do they answer our questions fully? What conclusions can we draw from the data we have collected? Could contrarians refute the conclusions based upon the same data, or are our interpretations inescapable? According to our readings and calculations, what would be a prudent next step? What action should we take now?

We should not fear data. There is no logical reason to fear information itself. The conclusions we draw, however, may give us ample cause to develop hives and tremors. But those fears are based upon the errors present in the activities prior to data collection. We shake because our reading program is ill-equipped to handle students of various backgrounds; we become anxious because we do not adequately differentiate our instruction for children of poverty; we grimace because a high percentage of students failed to complete simple algebraic equations correctly. These are not data-based fears; they are behavior-based fears. But the data show us what our shortcomings are and help us to devise a plan to overcome them.

Data are bits of information. Only when we scrutinize them and make sense of them do they take shape. Then, we become knowledgeable. Then we can act. Then we can succeed in our tasks. Don't you think it's time you found some data and thanked them for their presence and help?

Presentation Style: Medium, Double-Shot, Nonfat, with a Splenda

I attended a highly respected national education conference recently to build upon my own knowledge and expertise. I recognized a presenter's name from some terrific articles I'd read. The topic was one that interested me, and the session was positioned at a favorable time (after the morning coffee kicked in, but before the crash that followed my two apple fritters). Off I went, prepared to be mesmerized in a whirlwind of fabulous information and practical ideas to help me lead my school.

Fifteen minutes into the presentation: Zzzzzzz. We've all been there, haven't we? We're excited about a workshop only to be left nodding, doodling, and texting while a well-intentioned professional drones on without the least amount of acknowledgement that there's an audience in the room.

For the attendee and the presenter, I have two pieces of advice:

1. Attendee: Get up and leave. Show some respect for your own professional learning, your time, and the

money you spent to be there. If it's that bad, it's okay to get up and find something better to do. Chances are good that you're not learning anything anyway. Exiting is preferable to slumping into your chair and writing grocery lists.

2. Presenter: Get your act together! Show some respect for your colleagues' professional learning, their time, and the money they spent to be there. Lectures and monotonous ramblings do not further our profession. Spend a couple of minutes reading the rest of this essay to help your presentations shine.

Wanted: Best Practices

What do we know about presentation skills? From a participant's point of view, we know a lot. We want to be engaged. We want relevant information. We want to relate to our presenter, we want to enjoy learning, and we want some time to reflect and create a plan of action. We want presenters to utilize best practices in presentation skills.

There are enough captivating presenters out there to use as models. Look up individuals like Todd Whitaker (a superb speaker with a quick wit and a fantastic sense of humor), Marcia Tate (a master of engaging adult learners), Betty Hollas (a veteran educator who uses her flamboyant personality and stories to teach adults), and Derek Cordell (whose common-sense approach and self-deprecating sense of humor appeal to all audiences).

What can we do to engage our adult learners in convention seminars, staff meetings, professional development workshops, data analysis sessions, or any other gathering at which we'd like to tap into our people's best and most energy, inquisitiveness, and effort? Let's start here:

Relate to the audience. Don't picture them in their underwear because that just invites trouble. Instead, recognize them for who they are and the experiences they bring. Refer back to comments they've made, crack jokes, and value their contributions. This is professional development geared to deliver learning opportunities, after all. It's not an exercise in being professionally boring. If all you need is lecturing experience, go to Al's Hammer and Anvil Barn and practice with the miniature goats out back.

Have a sense of humor. There just isn't enough emphasis placed on the importance of comedy in professional development sessions. Laughter is the best medicine, and learning doesn't have to be a stressful, tedious event. Sometimes jokes (even lame ones) can lighten the mood and allow for a more relaxed environment. You don't have to be Gallagher smashing watermelons to be funny, either.

Engage the participants intentionally. Keep the participants involved with activities, give them opportunities to exchange ideas, provide time to manipulate thoughts, and offer chances to make the learning relevant through experience. Ask them to sing, to dance, to mime, to role-play, to switch places, to team up, to learn the ASL signs for vocabulary, to draw, to create a mind-movie, or to design a banner with key ideas. Recruit the participants to more actively participate in the learning. The active body stimulates an active brain and will help solidify the learning.

Tell stories. We know from all the research on best practices in schools that providing examples, making connections, and bringing the learning to life will help it settle into the participants' brains more efficiently. Plus, stories are fun and don't have to be real for people to remember their lessons. Have any good parables? Use them. Allegories? Fables? Tall tales? These are priceless tools for the well-equipped presenter.

Be personable. "Uncle Walter" Cronkite explained once that he delivered news broadcasts like he was talking to his mother in the living room. We're all regular people, and we'd like our key presenter to be a regular person, too. It builds credibility, it strengthens relationships, and it increases the respect so vital to receiving the message.

Rein in your PowerPoint. You know the rules, don't you? I read a commonsense piece of advice on a Web site this afternoon:

You are the presenter, not PowerPoint. With that in mind, KISS (Keep It Simple, Stupid):

♦ Only type your main points.
♦ Keep the font big enough to see from the back corner where most educators sit.
♦ Use pictures.
♦ Don't write 500 words and then read it to us in a monotone voice.
♦ Forget the special effects.

After all, the audience will have come to learn from you, not to read your book, listen to you read it to them, or to become dizzy following the exiting graphics. Pictures, graphics, and videos can be mesmerizing when used appropriately to support an idea, to illustrate a concept, or to infuse humor. Your PowerPoint presentation should be an aide, not the main event.

Give time for reflection and planning. My former colleague, co-author, and co-presenter Alisa Simeral, a dynamic and captivating presenter herself, wrote with me that the ability to self-reflect is directly related to our effectiveness. Ergo, we in the audience need time to consider, evaluate, analyze, and construct meaning. Then, once we've come to grips with the ideas, we could use a little bit of time to figure out how they're going to fit into our current reality. All too often we get good information then whisk ourselves to the next task, and the good information sits in a fancy steno pad awaiting the inevitable trip to the recycling bin. I conclude every one of my professional-development workshops, seminars, and presentations with a simple goal-setting form I've created called a "Now What?" I ask attendees to make a concrete plan—and write it down—if there's anything they'd like to change, improve, or focus on as a result of the time they just spent learning and working together. Plan it and it will happen!

Professional learning is vital. We cannot improve if we do not learn, do more, and achieve better than we are currently. We need help from our professional developers, no matter what role or arena they take. This list ought to get us rolling toward a day in which we can learn, grow, and develop with vigor, zest, excitement, and good cheer. Pass the Splenda.

Dog Training and American Schools

Sandwiching my *fun* reads—Lynne Cox's *Grayson* and *How to Survive Your New Siberian Husky Puppy*—this past month were a couple of retreads: a *Wall Street Journal* interview with New York City Department of Education chancellor Joel Klein (11/24/08) and a *Time* magazine article profiling the chancellor of the District of Columbia Public Schools, Michelle Rhee (12/08/08). I was captivated from the moment that I read the titles of those articles ("Failing Our Children" and "Can She Save Our Schools?" respectively).

At first I winced remembering what fates eventually befell these educational leaders. Were those articles simply adding to the barrage of American school bashing? As a current practitioner, an active principal in the American public school system, I bristle at negative press that propagates the assumption that our schools are broken, that the system is experiencing a cataclysmic meltdown. Can we please stop heaping criticism on perhaps the most delicate and vital component of our grander community?

Soon, however, I came to my senses. Perhaps it was my alarm clock or maybe it was my Siberian Husky whining at the door. Or maybe it was simply the resurgence of reality. Shoot! Our school system *is* struggling. Yes, there are pockets of excellence all around us, but as a whole we find ourselves on the short end of the measuring stick many times over.

We've heard the statistics. American students score well below most other countries in international measurements of reading and math proficiency across grade levels. Our graduates are ill-prepared to enter a competitive global society. We lack the number and percentage of math and science experts to continue our position as intellectual leaders. Our dropout rates are staggering. It's enough to make a dog want to move back to Siberia.

So there I was, walking my pup down the snowy streets while considering the mess we're in. I "thinked and I thunk 'til my thinker was sore" (Dr. Seuss, 1989), so I stopped to train the heterochromiatic-eyed dog (one hazel eye, one blue). We worked on "sit," "stay," "down," and "get the neighbor's cat," and then it came to me. If we really want to fix the American school system, we need to approach it more like training a puppy. Or, rather, a kennel of puppies—a gigantic, 50-million puppy kennel.

Training Point 1: Set up training sessions as often as possible. China, Japan, Germany, and Australia all significantly out-scored the United States in the 2006 Program for International Assessment (PISA) administration in math and science. Each one of those nations sends its children to school for over 200 days per year. Meanwhile, the United States still follows the 1847 Prussian model, based on the agricultural calendar, with a mere 180 school days (or fewer) per annum. Coincidence? Maybe. One piece of the puzzle? Surely. But if you want to teach your dog to "stay" or "shake," or if you want to teach your kids to develop scientific thinking proficiency, you'd better devote some serious time to it.

Training Point 2: Use each command consistently. It's no sur-prise that the standards-based movement has met little resis-tance philosophically. Who could argue against the idea that we should have clear definitions of our learning targets for students, educators, and parents to comprehend? When I tell my Husky to "sit," I expect him on his haunches sharpish, not lying down, crouching, or leaping. Every time, it's the same command, the same behavior, and the same issuance of a treat. Can you imagine his confusion, and the mass chaos that would ensue throughout the kennel if I rewarded dogs who made any sort of movement after I made my "sit" command? Or, even more damaging, if I took my puppy and "trained" him without any commands or expectations at all? And worse still, if my daughters came out and repeated the same inconsistent training approach? That's essentially what we're doing by allowing each state to have its own set of standards, its own assessment tool to measure student achievement, and its own criteria to determine success (i.e., Adequate Yearly Progress). Let's embrace the Common Core Standards as a consolidation of our massive knowledge base, utilize consistent assessment tools, and wield a common measuring stick. Then we can dig into the bag of treats with confidence.

Training Point 3: Only use good trainers. I took my Husky to obedience classes only to find the trainer negative, grumpy, and ill-tempered. As a responsible pet owner, it wasn't long before I realized this situation was headed nowhere, and we left for a new class and new trainer. The impact of a positive, effective, relationship-driven trainer is monumentally helpful, whereas the devastating effects of a negative trainer can cause irreparable damage to a dog. Funny, if the pup had been my son at the neighborhood school, I would have had far less leverage to remove him from an ineffective teacher's class—and we know that the damage a poor teacher can inflict is debilitating at best. In what other profession is career tenure awarded after as little as a year or two? In what other profession is it so excruciatingly difficult to remove an ineffective practitioner? In what other profession is the pay scale set up solely on the basis of longevity, with nary a glance toward merit? In what other profession is the salary so meager, anyway? We need to keep and reward top-notch professional teachers and redesign our system to more easily remove the harmful, damaging ones.

Training Point 4: Practice operant conditioning. We don't beat our dogs when they misbehave; we encourage them and reward them for doing well. Research from noted experts urges us to refrain from shoving a dog's snout in a living-room accident, informing us instead to provide the pooch with more frequent opportunities to go outside as well as rewards for doing his business in a designated spot in the backyard. Along the same lines, let's stop beating our schools when they under-perform. Let's see if we can get them the help and support they need to reach reasonable goals, then acknowledge their growth and progress. The theory behind operant conditioning is that we will receive more of what we expect when we reward it immediately. Meanwhile, those unwanted behaviors will dissipate if they are ignored, the reward is withheld, and the expectation is repeated. If my little Husky can get on board with this, I'm sure the well-educated professionals in our schools can embrace it also.

Chancellors Klein and Rhee had a common mission, a goal that should be uniting us all: the drastic improvement of our schools and school system. Some of the ideas I've outlined in this essay are congruent with their thinking, and I'm sure if they have dogs they would bark in agreement. If we really want to better our education system, we need to make it a priority and put our money where our mouths are.

It's not school-bashing or system-maligning if we point out our shortcomings and follow up by providing options and alternatives for growth, correct? As educators, we have an obligation to get involved. Write your senators and legislators. Contact an advocacy group. Get involved. Organize a march with your own puppy as you take a public stance. Millions of American students depend on us.

REFLECTION QUESTIONS

In Part II, you wrapped your arms around the idea of welcoming change as a positive element in your life, both personally and professionally. What's your next step? Use the following questions to guide your thinking about the ideas presented in Part II and the strategies you'll employ to implement them to motivate yourself or others. Then make it happen.

1. Think about a professional change that frustrated you recently. How did you handle the change? How did others respond to the change? What actions did you take to give the change a positive spin, no matter how you personally felt about it?
2. Consider the last professional development initiative that your school district launched. What steps worked to acquire buy-in from the staff? What was missing? How can you incorporate the lessons learned from that event into the next proposal you present to your staff and team?
3. What is the difference between delivering a thoroughly planned lesson and "winging it" in a classroom? How is

that different or similar to a principal leading a staff meeting? A department chair leading a collaborative session? A superintendent addressing the school board?

4. What structure do you currently have in place to reflect upon your work and your professional decisions? Do you have a trusted colleague or a critical friend with whom you can discuss, probe, challenge, and suggest courses of action? Consider setting up a structure in which you intentionally self-reflect on a regular basis.

5. Imagine that you have roughly one million things to do at work. (That was easy, wasn't it?) How do you prioritize your time, energy, and efforts? What items tend to make their way to the top of your to-do list? If you were in charge of your own time, energy, and efforts, what items would you move to the top? If you're not in charge of your own time, energy, and efforts, who is?

6. Pull out your school policies, your student handbook, or your classroom rules. How often are the words "don't," "avoid," and "never" included? Practice rewriting these items with positive phrasing. How does the meaning change? The tone? The expected outcomes?

7. Think back to the last time you changed jobs. What was your induction process? What advice were you given? Did you follow it or ignore it? Why?

8. "Change is the nature of the business." Why is this an important perspective in education? Do you agree with it or not? What lesson might this teach us about motivating ourselves or others?

9. How can you encourage the people you lead or influence to try something new? What strategies can you employ to share the acceptability of rough drafts, of implementation dips, of initial failures? Furthermore, how can you ensure that your people will stay on course?

PART III

Supera Diem

My rudimentary understanding of Latin (along with my Aunt Mary, a former college Latin professor at Mount Holyoke College in Massachusetts) tells me that the term "supera diem" means "survive the day." That's good advice to offer a building principal, a superintendent, lead teacher, department head, or any other type of educational leader. But what exactly should we do when we face the angry, clawing beast that rises in front of us every morning—the massive weight of the job itself—and doesn't seem to give us a chance to breathe, let alone enjoy an uninterrupted lunch break? Where is the practicality in a generic piece of advice like "supera diem," anyway? When you walk out the front door to get into the car on a particularly rainy, windy, and meeting-filled Monday morning, does your wife wave you good-bye with a wink and call out, "Supera diem, sweetheart," and then do you feel equipped to handle whatever life hurls at you?

I think not. In itself, it's clever, handy, and facile, but it's also woefully incomplete. Every day is an event unto itself. Most days move along quite satisfactorily, some even swimmingly. But how about those agonizing, torturous days that make us question our very existence? I say this: When you're in the mire, turn your mind to something glorious.

Think, for a moment, about a great day from your own life. Locate in your memory bank a day that was particularly memorable for a reason. Maybe it was a special event, like a wedding, birth, or ceremony. Perhaps it was during a vacation, a trip, or an adventure of some sort. What were the details?

Try to locate each and every minute particle of that day. Now transport yourself back to that place.

What a day, eh? Isolate and identify the emotions you're feeling, now that you're back there in that wondrous, amazing day. What are your senses telling you? What kinds of input do you receive from your surroundings, your companions, your inner self? Relish this experience. Wow! What a day.

Now come back to the present. Wouldn't it be fantastic if we could revisit that day, those moments, and conjure up those same emotions *whenever we wanted to*? What if we could control such things? What would that mean for our lives as we trudge along, day after day, conducting our business and playing out our existence? What would that mean for our lives on those disastrous, trying, frustrating, and merciless days that infect us every once in a while (or, for the unfortunate among us, *often*)? I believe we can.

The day I thought of was an ordinary winter day in 1984. I was 12 years old, living in Corvallis, Oregon—home of the Oregon State University Beavers. That year, I drew 11 × 17 inch pictures of each of the OSU men's basketball team's players, and they were delivered to the team through mutual connections. One Thursday afternoon, I hopped off the school bus and ran inside for a bowl of cereal. Honey Nut Cheerios, as I recall. It was cloudy, but not raining.

Why do I remember all of those details? Because right around 5:00 that evening, the phone rang. I answered after the second ring. On the other end of the line, clear as day and jettisoning me from my little life into orbit around our entire universe, was OSU basketball star A.C. Green. During our conversation that lasted all of four minutes, he complimented my artwork, talked with me about my parents and my future, and we chatted about basketball. Then we hung up.

For a 12-year-old, skinny kid who stood at a 45-degree angle to shoot free throws because that's how A.C. Green shot them, this was a spellbinding moment. For the rest of that day, heck, for the rest of that *year*, I bounded from cloud to cloud, shooting crooked free throws and marveling at the generosity and wonder offered by Mr. Green.

Later, Mr. Green went on to the NBA, set the league record for most consecutive games played, was an all-star, won three championships, had a fan for life, and wrote a book, *Victory:*

The Principles of Championship Living. In it, he describes the scene after getting pummeled by the upperclassmen at his college, both physically and mentally, during his first trip as a shy but confident freshman while playing pick-up basketball:

> Those guys were not just three-times better athletes. They were also ten-times better talkers, totally intimidating me with their 'trash talk' as much as with their play. I wondered if I could compete. When I went to the pros, I felt the same way. You have a gut check. You ask yourself, Can I play at this level? Mentally you can be telling yourself that you can do it. You know you have to go out there. Your faith can be really high, but there comes a time when you're just there. The battle lines are drawn. You're face-to-face with your opponent. Then you confront the moment of truth. Can you do it? (p. 54)

We all experience those days. Those are the ones that involve self-doubt, trepidation, uncertainty, nerves, dread, and perhaps a little knee-knocking fear. A first step in confronting our demons, in attacking the day, and in persisting through turmoil is to change our attitude. There's no sense in getting all gloomy about a rough situation, an interminable meeting, or a patch of bumpy road. Find the rose hiding out in all those thorns, that's what I always say.

In his national bestseller, *The Last Lecture,* Carnegie Mellon professor Randy Pausch explained his mindset as he approached every day, before and after learning that he had terminal pancreatic cancer:

> I don't know how not to have fun. I'm dying and I'm having fun. And I'm going to keep having fun every day I have left. Because there's no other way to play it.
>
> I came to a realization about this very early in my life. As I see it, there's a decision we all have to make, and it seems perfectly captured in the Winnie-the-Pooh characters created by A.A. Milne. Each of us must decide: Am I a fun-loving Tigger or am I a sad-sack Eeyore? Pick a camp. I think it's clear where I stand on the great Tigger/Eeyore debate. (pp. 179–180)

Another perspective, equally helpful and laden with optimism, is that of Dr. Spencer Johnson. Johnson's books, like *Who Moved My Cheese?* and *The One-Minute Teacher*, for instance, have been very helpful in developing some of my perspectives on the profession. In his engaging parable, *The Present*, Dr. Johnson describes the benefits of becoming fully immersed in what you're doing *right now*:

> The young man recalled talking with the old man about mowing lawns when he was a boy. He remembered how he had focused on cutting the grass and had not let anything else distract him.
>
> 'When you are fully engaged in what you are doing your mind doesn't wander. You enjoy life. And you are happier and more effective. You are intent only on what is happening at that moment. And that focus and concentration leads to your success.'
>
> He realized he had not felt that way for a long time—about work or anything else. He spent too much time being upset about the past or worried about the future. (p. 34)

In the essays that follow, you'll be challenged to look at each day through a new lens. Whether it's finding that little piece of encouragement in your life (like in "Who's Your Joey Amalfitano?") or convincing yourself and others to raise the ceiling (such as in "57 Games"), you may find a nugget of inspiration while you're dredging your river of life. No matter how you read and receive them, you're sure to be more likely to survive each day with more vigor, more enthusiasm, and more optimism. Perhaps A.C. Green will even call you to congratulate your efforts. *Supera diem*, sweetheart!

Making It Fun Again

Today it hit you: You're the CEO (Chief Everything Officer) at your school, and as much as you love your job, you're beginning to feel a bit down. So far down, in fact, that you seem to be looking up at the Mohorovicic discontinuity. But why is that? What's the deal?

It's HULA time!

The following list of symptoms might help you determine if you're in need of a HULA (Hopeful Unwavering Lighthearted Approach):

- ◆ Exhausted at your list of responsibilities as principal?
- ◆ Frustrated at the lack of funding support for your school?
- ◆ Baffled by the students' zany behaviors and work ethic?
- ◆ Irritated by the barrage of overbearing parents at your door?
- ◆ Appalled by the negative press in the papers?
- ◆ Handcuffed by the teachers union's influence?
- ◆ Saddened by the dearth of professionalism around you?
- ◆ Pummeled by the list of demands from the central office?
- ◆ Confused by college football's BCS rankings?
- ◆ Forgotten what your spouse and kids look like?

If any of the above symptoms match what you jot in your diary every night (after checking 67 new e-mails, completing a report, writing a teacher's observation summary, making two parent phone calls, planning for a budget committee meeting, and trying to make sense of your day), you're not alone.

Chances are, if you're feeling exhausted, frustrated, or baffled, the folks surrounding you are, too. The teachers are grumpy. The parents are snotty. The support staff are cranky. The children are unwieldy. The carpets are crusty. Remember: The principal sets the mood. If you're cantankerous and grouchy, it's contagious.

Remember This, Too

We're working in schools, for heaven's sake. We're working with children. We're working with people who have devoted their lives to work with children. We're working with people who have dedicated themselves to helping children learn and grow. What's not fun about children? Just watch them for a little while. It doesn't matter if the children are six, sixteen, or sixty-seven; the mission is the same, and we should have fun achieving it.

As we embrace the HULA concept, our gait transforms from trudging down the driveway in the morning to skipping through the hallways. We separate our eyebrows again. Sullen waves turn to cheerful high-fives. Exasperation morphs into exhilaration.

But how does that happen? What do we do?

Fun Ain't a Four-Letter Word

Do you have a sense of humor? Sometimes, a good remedy for our malaise is some good old-fashioned, light-hearted fun. If you have a good sense of humor, quit stifling it. Tell some jokes. If you're a bit stodgier, ask a colleague to share some jokes. Put them in the school newsletter. Tell them over the P.A. system. (Write them on a "graffiti board" in the staff restroom if they're not child-friendly.) Laughter is the best medicine, after all, and we could use a dose or two.

Create some fun, special days at the school. Children (and adults) love dress-up days—you know, those days with a novel theme. Encourage school, team, or community spirit by scheduling Funny Hat Day, Wrong Shoe Day, or Superhero Day. You'll be amazed at the results, especially if there's some sort of contest attached to it.

Celebrate positive accomplishments. Start each staff meeting (or any other get-together) with good news. Clap. Recognize all the good things that are happening out there. Toot some horns, for crying out loud. Loudly bellow some shout-outs for deserving deeds. Acknowledge the students and their feats publicly, privately, in assemblies, or in phone calls to parents. Let's start sharing the good stuff.

Plan some giveaways. Recruit local merchants and businesses to partner in goodie giveaways. Even if it's small—like a free coffee, a month's supply of dry-cleaning, or a replica rodeo belt buckle, or a Mini Cooper—a little treat handed out to an unsuspecting individual can make the recipient's week. The businesses will appreciate being included, too, so it's a win-win.

Practice random acts of zany behavior. Go on the playground and play with the children. Wear something unorthodox. Dance. Lead an assembly from the school rooftop or atop a fire engine. Borrow a wig. Or better yet, borrow a handful of different wigs and change them throughout the day. Keep your staff on their toes, give them something to discuss rather than grumble about (you can control the topic du jour!), and generate some enthusiasm. Then, wait. It's likely that other staff members will follow suit.

Make a list of what you love about your work. Recalibrate your mission. Ask your staff to do the same. Jot those items on a 3 × 5 card and keep it in your pocket, your wallet, or pinned to the corkboard by your desk. When we isolate what we enjoy, and when we focus on the good parts, we're more likely to continue to enjoy them. Love and happiness beget more love and happiness. It's a wonderful cycle.

Take care of yourself. Eat broccoli. Exercise. Get enough sleep. Take your vitamins. Pet your dog. Drink enough water. Practice yoga. Spend time with friends. Take up a non-principalship-related hobby. Do the activities that you enjoy. You'll find yourself having a lot more fun engaging in those activities when you dedicate yourself to them. And, in turn, you'll find that the happiness within spreads to your work-related duties and to everything else.

All of Those Shiny Teeth Can't Be Wrong

There are 500 students in my school. We have roughly 70 staff members. Counting the lost-incisors and scrutinizing the maxillas and mandibles of all those folks, we're looking at roughly, well, a lot of teeth. Why aren't they all part of wide, toothy grins? Remember: The faces of the people under your charge act like a giant, circus house mirror. They reflect what you project.

Yes, there's plenty of work to do. Yes, the checklist at the beginning of this essay is common for principals. Yes, you'll still encounter crabby colleagues, parents, students, lawyers, teachers, and deli-counter workers. But when you're prepared with a steady diet of fun-loving strategies, you can turn those frowns upside-down. You, too, can act as a HULA-inducing agent for those around you.

Who's Your Joey Amalfitano?

Have you ever had one of those days? You know the kind: You wake up late, you burn the toast, the cat vomited on the rug (you find out by stepping in it), you leave the house just barely behind schedule but then have to stop for gas, you get to school just in time to remember you had a meeting with a parent that started 15 minutes ago—and it doesn't get much better after that.

We all experience those days, and we all fight with ourselves to figure out how to combat them. Short of inventing a time machine and going back 24 hours so you can try the entire thing again, what do you do? Answer this forced-choice question by choosing one:

A. Wallow in freakish misery
B. Go home, pour yourself a warm (to the throat) beverage, and take a nap
C. Seek out your Joey Amalfitano

Who? Good question. Were you confused about option C? Who's Joey Amalfitano? And more important, who's *your* Joey Amalfitano? For help, let's consult with Hall of Fame baseball player Willie Mays, who recounts a special story in his autobiography, *Say Hey: The Autobiography of Willie Mays*.

In 1961, Mr. Mays was having a terrific season for the San Francisco Giants, but was mired in a terrible slump. One day, after eating some bad ribs and falling very ill the night before, he came to the ballpark sick, wretched, and unable to play.

Enter friend and teammate Joey Amalfitano, a career .244 hitter with just one home run when he entered the 1961 season. He was a little guy with a charm far exceeding his muscle.

Before the game, Joey grinned and lent big Mr. Mays his little bat suggesting that he try using it to overcome the sickness and end the slump. Mr. Mays reluctantly obliged.

After unexpectedly drilling one ball after another over the fence in batting practice, Mr. Mays excitedly begged the manager to keep him in the lineup. That game, he slugged a record-tying four home runs, en route to a 40-homer season. Without the impromptu inspiration from his diminutive teammate, Mr. Mays may have ended up sitting out that game!

A Source of Inspiration

Sometimes leadership and inspiration come from places we don't expect. When Mr. Mays was down and (almost) out, he could have gone back home, had a drink, and retreated to bed. Or he could have sat dejectedly in the dugout, wallowing in freakish misery. But instead he ran into Joey Amalfitano.

Maybe it was blind luck. Maybe it was fortune. Maybe he subconsciously sought out Joey as a trusted source of optimism and good humor. Who knows? Whatever the impetus or cause may have been, the effect was the same: Joey Amalfitano was the cure for all that ailed Mr. Mays that day.

Take a few moments and ponder the days when it seems the very earth and sky are out to get you. Everything that could possibly go wrong has befallen you. The students are all out of sorts, and it seems all you're doing is discipline. Parents have formed a line to scream, berate, and attack you. You've got a mountain of paperwork so high it has clouds atop it, and your to-do list has just extended onto your fifteenth Post-It note. It's definitely, unquestionably, indubitably, and incontrovertibly *one of those days.*

Think of your options, because to make a decision about how to respond to these events is the one thing that's under your control. If you were to select A or B from the quiz above, what would the result have been?

Choose A: You're likely to bring down everyone who interacts with you, talks to you, or even sees you from a distance. That day becomes a plague, which you spread with your own toxic attitude. The day, in turn, goes from bad to worse to ghastly.

Choose B: This is likely to extend the length of the cruddy day because when you wake up, you have a headache, you've missed a meal, and you realize that when you get back to work you have at least two days of work to make up. The oblivion gets darker.

Choice C is the logical response. Find what works for you to get your groove on. Maybe it's a friend. Maybe it's a song. Maybe it's a task that immerses you. Maybe it's a snack—a healthful snack, to be sure, like broccoli, V-8 juice, or apple-cinnamon rice cakes. Whatever it is, take some time to engage in some self-reflection and find out: *Who's your Joey Amalfitano?*

Educators (and, for that matter, mere mortal humans as well) have sought out, encountered, and implemented all sorts of strategies to de-funk these days, Amalfitano style. Some go for a walk around the campus. Others visit that one first-grade class in which the teacher is always doing everything just right, there's soothing music in the background, and the children are happy and peaceful. Some may watch a short clip from the Onion News Network to bring a smile to their faces. Others may just duck into the staff restroom to try out a new hairstyle. And some, of course, visit, call, text, e-mail, Skype, or write a letter to that person who always seems to know how to bring them out of it. Yup, it's their Joey Amalfitano.

The next time you have one of those days, seek out your choice C. Force your attitude to get the better of your frustration. The options are endless if you take the time and put forth the effort. If all else fails, remember the valuable lesson Johnny Cash's shoeshine boy taught us all of those years ago: "Get rhythm when you get the blues."

The Upside

They say, "Every cloud has a silver lining," but I have a couple of questions about that. Who are "they," anyway? And do they know anything about the composition of clouds? These accumulations of water droplets or ice crystals floating in the troposphere really have no relation to the metallic chemical element found in our forks and spoons, do they?

A scientist friend of mine smirked across a buffet at the Silver Nugget Casino somewhere in the Silver State (Nevada) one day when I asked him that, and he responded: "Well, maybe not every cloud, but the ones that are seeded to produce rain are laced with silver iodide." That wasn't yet a plausible enough explanation, so I remained skeptical.

Then, a teacher friend of mine guffawed as we drove past the Silver Cloud Inn on a cloudy day in Silver City, Nevada, explaining, "It's an idiom. That's figurative language. It means there's usually something good, even in what appears to be a terrible situation." After I realized she wasn't calling me names, I officially became a believer.

Actually, the idea of finding the positive in every situation has always been appealing to me. I was raised (though we call it "cursed") a fourth-generation diehard fan of the Boston Red Sox, whose remarkable 86-year World Series championship drought was well-chronicled from 1918 until 2004. That means my father, grandfather, and great-grandfather all experienced the same demoralizing punch line to the same tantalizing joke, autumn after autumn, even when the Sox had teased us all summer long with strong seasons, great players, and terrific ballpark franks.

Singin' in the Rain

In our lives, we all run into obstacles, those days that start poorly and get worse with each tick of the clock. Somebody or other acts as our "enemy," perhaps a disgruntled coworker, a micro-managing boss, an unhappy spouse, an incompetent employee, or an inconsiderate driver. Our plans are interrupted, our ideas are thwarted, our intentions are blunted, and our actions are erroneous. In short, our lives are ruined. Or at least that's how it might seem from the inside. Let's consider what actions we can take to counteract the negative forces acting upon us to find that glorious silver lining in each thunderhead that threatens our very existence.

Shift perspective. What if we were to look at adversity as an opportunity, rather than a curse? In *The Art of Happiness,* His Holiness the Dalai Lama offers the perspective that "the enemy is the necessary condition for practicing patience." He goes on to explain that, "when you come across such a chance for practicing patience and tolerance, you should treat it with gratitude," for those virtues are critical in eliminating negative emotions. So thank you, Red Sox, for those decades of heartache and misery. Without that basis for comparison, the sweet nectar of victory would not have carried the same impact upon those of us who suffered for generations. Ask yourself this question: What can you gain from the predicament you're in?

Think flexibly. A necessary prerequisite for being able to view a problem from multiple vantage points—looking up from the rubble, viewing it on the same level at the ground floor, overseeing it from the balcony, and seeing it globally with an infrared satellite image—is to have a flexible mind. This is a skill we can develop. The next time a situation presents itself to you, take a few moments to reflect: How is this scenario different if I view it from so-and-so's perspective? Has a similar scene played out in my life before, and if so, what was the result? What might be some of the causes of this scenario? What might be the results if I choose path A, path B, or path C? Tackling adversity with an open mind, one pliable enough to accept varying view points, will strengthen your resolve to encounter the most welcoming solution.

Dig for it. Often, like in the case of a pearl hiding in an oyster, the rewards aren't in plain sight. Determining the upshot of a particularly rough position might take some work. So lace 'em up tight, buckle up, and put on your working gloves already! When the district office informs you that the school budget's been cut by 25 percent, and you had already garnered staff support for the projected expenditures through a rigorous and contentious process, what silver lining could possibly exist? After peeling back the layers and viewing this scenario from different angles, you realize that a chopped budget sheet provides you just the right excuse to veto a couple of items that certain staff members fought to have included, despite your rational pleas that they didn't necessarily match the school's mission statement. A gorgeously fortuitous chain of events, that's what I always say.

Commit to your goal(s). Failing is necessary. To fail or otherwise struggle forces us to decide what's really important.

What outcomes do we really want to realize? Will the long-term results outlast the immediate suffering? Take the curious case of one, Abraham Lincoln, for example. Here's a man who lost eight elections, yet through his persistence and dedication he eventually became a legendary U.S. President, leading the country in undoubtedly its most tumultuous era. When we run into a brick wall, we're faced with options. Change direction and chart a course toward a new destination, or truly commit to the original plan, going over, under, around, or through that insufferable wall.

Think optimistically. In *Failing Forward*, leadership uber-author John Maxwell shares the story of a research study on people who lost their jobs multiple times: "Psychologists expected them to be discouraged, but they were surprisingly optimistic." And why? Since they had gone through the muck before, they believed the next opportunity was right around the corner. That put positive thoughts in their minds, which allowed them to concentrate their efforts on achieving their goals. Imagine: Tomorrow will be a better day. I'll get my turn. This will get cleaned up. I can still do it.

Remain confident. The most important lesson to learn from adversity is that it happens to everyone. We've all lost items, been fired from jobs, received hate-mail of one form or another, endured verbal assaults from an angry fellow human, faced unachievable deadlines, or otherwise failed miserably at something. The greatest basketball player of all time, Michael Jordan, sums it up with this: "I've missed more than 9,000 shots in my career. I've lost almost 300 games. 26 times, I've been trusted to take the game winning shot and missed. I've failed over and over and over again in my life. And that is why I succeed." Now that's a silver lining.

Stop It!

A trusted and respected colleague of mine once introduced me to a problem-solving strategy she watched on an episode of "Mad TV." Now, wait a minute, just because she watches

"Mad TV" doesn't mean she can't be a trusted colleague and respectable individual. In fact, there are lots of things about "Mad TV" that can help develop one's critical thinking skills, deductive reasoning approaches, and professional capacity. Just because I can't think of one in particular doesn't mean it's not there, right?

Anyway, she told me of a skit in which the main character's response to aversive behaviors was to yell "Stop it!" at the offender. That's it. Just those two little words. It's contrary to the Nike philosophy and might even make Phil Knight jealous of its brevity, but sometimes succinct wins. And, anyway, Nancy Reagan would approve.

Wasting Time, Are We?

It comes to mind today because I'm struck by the amount of, um,—what's the word in English?—*crud* that we see in education today. We waste a lot of time. We put our energy in fruitless tasks. We focus on the wrong things. We leave precious moments hanging in the air, twisting on whatever breeze pushes them, and then lament our loss.

So how can we straighten ourselves out? How can we reclaim that time? How can we get the biggest bang for every tick of the clock? Time, after all, is our most prized commodity. And we often act as if there's a spare reservoir waiting for us to tap.

Remember that old joke about the fellow who walks into the hospital? Bending his arm back over his head in an awkward position, he says, "Hey doc, when I do this, my arm hurts." Then the doctor hands him a prescription that reads, "Stop doing that." At least that fellow knew the cause of his pain.

Many of us in education are sadly unaware of what distracts us from our real work. It takes introspection, reflection, and self-analysis to figure it out. We often don't think of *why* we've missed the boat; we just lament that we're still on shore, watching it sail away.

Our Prescription

It turns out there is a veritable cornucopia of reasons why we don't have enough time, why we don't get all our work done, and why our inbox is perpetually higher stacked than the out-box. We don't prioritize. We don't focus. We don't expend our energy on the right tasks. We don't maximize every second that's available to us. There is no spare reservoir, people. So if this sounds like you, and if you do any of the following tasks, there's some simple advice waiting for you:

Do you check and write e-mails during school hours? *Stop it!* You can only supervise teachers, monitor student learning, observe authentic instruction, and build relationships around campus during the time children are in class. The e-mails will still be there after school.

Do you listen to messages and make phone calls during school hours? *Stop it!* Just like e-mails, these messages will still be there after the children go home. And they'll be there tomorrow morning, strangely enough. I have a 24-hour rule: I'll get back to parents and other callers within 24 hours. Not within 24 seconds, or even 24 minutes. 24 hours. If it's more urgent than that, you'll hear a siren.

Do you sit at your desk and do paperwork? *Stop it!* Did you get into school administration to be a pencil-pusher? Are you affecting positive change by filling out forms and writing during the day? Do it later, do it earlier, or better yet: See if you can find someone else to do it! (That's not always appropriate, but if you find yourself in a situation where it's okay to delegate, go for it!)

Do you try to be everything to everyone? *Stop it!* It's hard to say "no," to keep walking when you've got a destination *and* a teacher trying to stop you for a quick question, but sometimes "no" is an acceptable answer. You don't have to know every-thing, do everything, be everywhere, and drop everything every time someone wants your ear (or your hide!). That's why we have calendars ("Let's schedule a meeting for later"), e-mail ("Send me your question and I'll get to it after school"), phone messages ("I'd like to hear your voice, just not now!"), and keys ("Scratch your message into the hood of my car and I'll get back to you *really quickly!*").

Do you go to too many "pointless" meetings? *Stop it!* Doug Reeves (in *The Learning Leader*, 2006) advises us to excuse ourselves from these time-wasters. If we have nothing to contribute, and if the meeting doesn't expand our knowledge or our potential, then we could better spend our time elsewhere. I'm a particular advocate against "talking memo" meetings, in which a series of visitors read a script to the audience. If that starts, just salute, smile, and walk.

Do you do other peoples' work? *Stop it!* There's a reason that I've dubbed Stephen Covey's Quadrant IV activities (from *The 7 Habits of Highly Effective People*, 1989) "handoffs." Other people should be doing them: standing in front of the copy machine, collating packets for a professional development workshop, standing in line for lunch, ordering materials online, organizing bookshelves, filing paperwork, changing light bulbs, and so forth. I know we wear a lot of hats as principals, but this is ridiculous!

Do you try to multitask and end up dilly-dallying? *Stop it!* We all need to have things that bring us joy and keep us mentally healthy. The principalship is one step shy of *One Flew over the Cuckoo's Nest*, so a little diversion is nice. But when we take some paperwork home or when we have reports to write and forms to complete, do we allow ourselves to get distracted by personal time killers? I've seen it time and again: someone may have all the best of intentions to get the work finished, but fiddling around on the side means the work doesn't get done. Online chat rooms, video games, television programs, personal e-mail, sports fantasy leagues, texting could all conceivably fit in the "personal happiness" column on your life's organizational chart, but only in reasonable doses. I suggest we eschew those behaviors and actions that don't contribute to our growth and progress. If you have something to do, do it and do only that task until it's complete.

Do you worry about things that are beyond your control? *Stop it!* We can admire all of our problems until the cows come home, but that won't help us address our most dire needs. Research studies tell us that students born prematurely are likely to be academically delayed; your district's Title I funding has been reapportioned and next year you will receive $50,000 less; parents just don't value education for their children anymore; our student mobility rate is climbing every year! There are a million reasons why our students *can't* succeed. We will help them realize success only when we create and implement a plan where they *can* succeeed. Worshiping factors outside our influence is a fruitless pursuit. And it gobbles up our time. With a little focus, some reflection, and personal willpower, we can create our own spare reservoir—before the time runs out. And as for each of those other things? Stop it!

Why I Wear Red Socks to School

The earliest known knit socks were discovered in Egyptian tombs dating from around 200 A.D. In the subsequent 1,800 years, socks have taken many turns on the paths of style and function. Mine, for instance, are red. Every day, I wear red socks. You, loyal reader, are not the first to ask the question, "Why?" Let me begin my response by explaining a couple of details:

◆ My red socks do not necessarily match anything else I am wearing.
◆ The socks are neither thicker nor thinner depending on the weather.
◆ I am not averse to donning soccer socks, dress socks, wool socks, softball socks, or even brand-name socks— as long as they're red.
◆ I have many pairs of socks, so don't worry about their scent or starchiness; they are clean.

I wear red socks only on school days and only if children will be present. If I am to attend a meeting or conference off-campus all day, I do not wear them unless, of course, I am speaking and wish to discuss the matter of my inner footwear with my audience.

I can sense you repeating, "Why?"

Ask Johnny Cash

I wear red socks for the same reason Johnny Cash always wore black. To paraphrase the late, great singer, I wear the socks "for the poor and the beaten-down/living in the hopeless, hungry side of town."

As a school principal, I work with hundreds of children every day. The life situations in which many of those children find themselves are rough—poverty, lack of parental engagement, single-parent homes, poor nutrition, drugs, incarceration, rough neighborhoods, gangs, loud dogs, bad music, rogue Yankees fans, and countless other factors. I work in a high-poverty neighborhood, but the troubles children bring with them to school are not exclusive to high-poverty neighborhoods by any means.

School also comes at them hard—deadlines, demands, schedules, assignments, discipline, expectations, social systems, and lockers that jam just for the sake of jamming during passing times. Imagine how a child feels while trying to navigate this harsh labyrinth some days. My thought is this: Flash 'em some sock.

I can't tell you the number of times I've encountered a sad child on the playground, upset at the way her mother screamed at her that morning. I've tried consoling her in various tried-and-true ways, to no avail. She's heartbroken, dejected, and terribly upset. Then I attempt a different tactic: In the course of our subsequent conversation I've typically said something like, "Well, at least you're not wearing red socks . . ." That usually draws a wry grin—or at least a puzzled look—which I can capitalize on. Then I can begin working with this child on some positive thoughts and strategies for handling life's bummer moments.

Ask the Guy Shaving His Head or Dropping Out of a Helicopter

We've all read in the newspaper, or heard from our colleagues, about the school principal who set a goal for the students and promised them, "If you read 1,000 books this year, I'll shave my head, paint it like a soccer ball, and rappel out of a helicopter during recess." Our first instinct is to raise our eyebrows a bit, snort, and say, "What a nut."

The children at that school, however, will remember that nut. Or, more specifically, they will remember that nut's crazy, snort-inducing stunt. Forever.

The short-term benefits of such a (zany, wild, extravagant, memorable) promise are clear: increased motivation for the students to achieve a goal, to meet a standard, to accomplish a task, to slay a dragon; amplified attention for a challenge, a cause, a purpose.

The long-term benefits, perhaps rarely considered, run parallel to my red socks. The students will remember the stunt, they will remember my socks, they will remember the principal sitting in the dunk-tank with lime-green dyed hair. Then they will remember (brace yourself): school.

In 20 years, a couple of old classmates will be sitting around a campfire, enjoying a bottle of water or two, and this conversation may ensue:

"Hey, remember that principal with the red socks?"

"Yeah, the one with the skinny head and pointy ears?"

"What was his name?"

"I don't know, but that school was awesome."

"I know, that's when we met. Remember when Adam brought the snake to school and it escaped . . ."

The socks are simply a prop in the playhouse. The socks will jog the students' memories about their school days, bringing up recollections of the good times, the great times, and the times in between. The expectation is that they will then pass along those good feelings and stories to their children, thereby enhancing the positive relationship with school itself, and perhaps even strengthening the family bond.

Is It the Socks?

The socks, by themselves, are immaterial. Some may say I wear red socks because I'm a Boston Red Sox baseball fan. That's actually true—that was the original inspiration behind the socks for me, but any school principal can pick up any little gimmick, gadget, or hooyah that can capture their students' imagination and burn a positive image into their memory banks.

Then, whether the students start by remembering "the principal with the earrings," "the principal who stayed on the roof for two weeks," or "the principal who dressed like a gypsy," they'll finish by remembering all that was good about their school experiences.

So let's make those school experiences as positive as they'll want to remember.

57 Games

On May 15, 1941, Joltin' Joe DiMaggio hit a single in a baseball game against the Chicago White Sox. Big deal, right? Hall of Fame ballplayers have experienced more impressive offensive outputs than that. What makes that hit special, however, is that the seemingly innocuous base hit was the start of The Streak. The Yankee Clipper proceeded to get a hit in every game for an unprecedented—and as yet unmatched—56 games.

Yes, The Streak is one of baseball's most revered statistics. (This says a lot for a game in which a batter's on-base percentage vs. a left-handed pitcher in a night game on a Tuesday in July in a domed stadium during a bobble-head giveaway is actually accessible and shared with the TV audience.) Former baseball commissioner Ford Frick called it "unbeatable." The Baseball Almanac refers to it as "unbreakable." A New York Times article called it "baseball's most mythic achievement." Baseball purists generally agree that 56 is "untouchable."

I say, "Hogwash!"

I am a firm believer in the 57-game hitting streak. Sure, it hasn't happened yet (the closest was Pete Rose's 44-game streak in 1978), but it's a possibility, isn't it? Mr. Rose and I would bet on it. Who's to say that a record, even one as hallowed as DiMaggio's Streak, is the mark of absolute perfection, something that cannot be topped? For that matter, who's to say that anything of greatness can't be somehow improved upon, made better, enhanced, or outdone? Why can't there be a 57-game hitting streak?

Do the Can-Can

As I work and talk with educators around the country, I'm struck by how often I still hear the sighing lines . . .

◆ "We can't do that here."
◆ "Not with our _____ (fill in the blank: staff, demographics, principal, PTA, teachers' union, violence, superintendent, parking lot, etc.)."
◆ "That wouldn't work with these kids."
◆ "We've squeezed as much blood as we can out of this turnip."

Why *can't* we do it here? Seriously: Why not?

Whenever I hear the word *can't,* I try to figure out if there's a *can* in there.

Have you heard of Lorraine Monroe, who revitalized the Fredrick Douglass Academy in New York City? What about Erin Gruwell? Rick DuFour? Ron Clark? Charlie Coleman? You may recognize those names because they're educators who have made remarkable progress and achieved incredible results in challenging educational environments. Those people have framed their lives around the word "can."

In fact, there are enough examples of against-the-odds teachers and principals out there that we should be continuously inspired to reach (and surpass) the high bars they've set for us. Some might call them "Superman." Others might claim they're just "positive deviants." I posit that they're more prevalent and available than we know. Truly, the models are available for us to follow. The "can" is waiting.

Two Steps

I see two steps that we can all take:

Find the models and share them! We need to come to grips with the fact that the well-known educators we read and hear about (in education journals, at conferences, and on made-for-TV specials) are but a minute sampling of the hordes of superb teachers and principals we have roaming our schools and classrooms. Perhaps we just don't have enough of them who are willing to share the great work they're doing so that we can follow their lead!

When you hear, observe, or do work that exceeds normal expectations or realizes terrific results, encourage the parties responsible to share it. Tell them to write, post, blog, shout, or present. It's an obligation to the profession to share such best-practices; it's not braggadocio. Like Dizzy Dean, Hall of Fame pitcher for the St. Louis Cardinals in the 1930s is supposed to have said, "It ain't braggin' if you really done it."

If you're looking for models to follow, do some digging to find schools similar to yours (in population or demographics, for example) that have excelled. Use websites such as www.allthingsplc.info, www.teachingasleadership.org, and www.EducationTrust.org to start your search. It's amazing how many great schools are out there with effective structures or elements that we can all emulate.

Remove the ceilings! The individuals listed above are not all Joe DiMaggios: They're just regular people like you and me. They just believed so fervently, so passionately, and so resolutely that they refused to accept anything less than excellence.

That, my friends, is replicable. We can all embrace the can-do attitude that leads to breakthroughs and astonishing success. In our dreams, in our ultimate realities, and in our visions of the future, all things are possible. We don't deflate our wishes and ambitions by placing artificial ceilings atop them. We strive for perfection—or at least continued improvements. We set goals that exceed what has been done before. We aim high, we raise the bar, we push the envelope because we know that when we believe, we can.

When you have a moment, walk into a classroom and look at the field of students growing in neat rows, clusters, or tables. Imagine amazing things for each one of them. Envision audacious successes, beyond even their wildest dreams. They deserve that from us—that unyielding expectation of greatness, and our attention to ensure that they achieve it.

Conversely, what if we settled? What if mediocrity were acceptable? What if the best we can do is what we've already done? What if we never wondered what we could really do if we applied everything we know and could learn? What if we never challenged the limits of our potential? We'd still be sitting in the cave, shivering in front of a pile of dry sticks, watching yet another deer wander by as we looked blankly at one another, that's what.

Go get that seemingly innocuous single and start your own 57-game hitting streak.

Seven Seconds

Today, my good readers, I have a challenge to issue:

Think of a child who holds special meaning to you. The child may be your son, granddaughter, niece, or your neighbor's darling little angel that stops by your house every afternoon asking for a Kit Kat. Imagine, if you will, that child's regular routines on a normal school day. Breakfast, backpack, out to the car, back to the house to put the other shoe on, back to the car, and off to school. Then think of the interactions this special child has with adults.

Odds are pretty good that this precious child had a good-morning hug and kiss from mom and/or dad, was encouraged to eat a healthy breakfast, received reminder (after reminder after reminder) to brush those pearly whites, engaged in some lighthearted conversation about baseball or goats or the solar system or the compositions of metals in a fork, snuck in an extra hug and kiss, then went bounding down the sidewalk like Tigger en route to Pooh's place for some honey. We ensure that the children dear to our hearts get their recommended daily allowances of love, encouragement, and preparation for each and every day.

For a tremendous number of children, however, Pooh's honey jars are empty.

Switch your thinking for a moment.

Consider the roughly one million American children who are victims of child abuse or neglect every year.

Ponder the ten million children in the U.S. who witness violence in their own homes this year.

Imagine the three million school-age children who have an incarcerated parent (or two incarcerated parents) *right now.*

We are talking about *millions* of children. And what about the kiddos who have less dire, but no less impactful, episodes of neglect and bullying, or feel worthless and disconnected? What do their mornings look like? How might they compare with the routines of the special child who you smiled about earlier?

Staying Positive

We know facts about the correlation between attitude and altitude: Positive thoughts lead to positive results. That's why
motivational sites like www.BucketFillers101.com exist, why
John Maxwell's books have sold a quindecillion copies (that's
an estimation, literally 10^{48}, but in layman's terms, it's "a heck-
uva lot"), and why Boston Red Sox fans held on for 86 years
until that elusive World Series championship finally arrived.
We agree that we must think positively, create positive images,
and act in a positive way. But where did we learn this? Why,
from those caring, doting, attentive, supportive adults.

If you're like me and you work in a school with hundreds
of children scampering and scuttling about all day long, you've
had a centillion opportunities (again, just ballparking, but that's
somewhere around 10^{303}) to watch the youngsters arrive at the
schoolhouse in the morning. Some disembark from warm vehi-
cles with the music of "I love you!" serenading them as blown
kisses chase their confident, happy, well-adjusted selves toward
the main entrance. Others get off a bus, laughing and giggling
with friends as they share stories of puppies, mittens, weekend
plans, and basketball scores.

And then there are our honey-free children. Downtrodden,
burdened, exhausted, overwhelmed, disenfranchised, lonely,
confused, battered, scared, anxious, or depressed they trudge
uncertainly toward the door. We watch them walk. We see the
scars in their expressions. The worry shrouds them like a morning fog. Our hearts ache, our empathy is activated, and our
concern heightens. "If only," we tend to think. "If only there
were something I could do. Poor thing." We watch them pass
without making eye contact, hardly even breathing. Then we
see them walk by a mysterious *someone* . . .

Seven Seconds Later

. . . and after a similarly mysterious interaction, those same
honey-free children crack a smile. Eyes glint. Shoulders
de-hunch. Steps become more sprightly. Britches get yanked
back up above the keister. Laughter fills the air. A child who just
seven seconds ago appeared broken and destined for disaster
now shows promise, life, and expression.

What just happened? A caring, dedicated adult just maximized the use of seven seconds. It only takes seven seconds to make a child's day. Seven seconds is all it takes to weave a little love into an ordinary, run-of-the-mill morning routine. Transforming the ordinary into the extraordinary, tending to a relationship, filling a need, answering a call, cheering a soul: This all takes just seven seconds.

During those seven seconds, that caring, dedicated, and not-so-mysterious someone could have said something like this: "Good morning, Jacoby! You look like you're ready for school today. Did you get a new haircut? Very handsome! Look out world, here comes the pride of Lion-town: Jacoby! Have a good day today, young man."

How long is seven seconds? Have you ever watched a pretty fast baseball player hit a double? It takes about seven seconds to run from home plate to second base. Seven seconds might be but a blip to you (it's roughly 0.008 percent of a 24-hour day), but it could last a lifetime in the experience of a child. It's a small investment on our part to fill a bucket, to infuse some positive energy, to generate some forward momentum, and to set in motion events that change lives. And since it doesn't take too long and it isn't terribly complicated to implement, a seven second investment is a relatively easy way to make a humongous difference in the world of a child, a family, a group, a class, or an entire school.

Making It Happen

You can make it happen! Just . . .

Be there. A prerequisite to dedicating seven seconds to this cause is to be where the children are. Good places might include the cafeteria, the bus line, the front entryway, the main hallways, the playground, the library, the corner crosswalk—anywhere you might find children, especially those who you know are in need of some heavy-duty bolstering.

Take the initiative. Go ahead and be the first one to say, "Good morning!" and offer a hand for a high-five, or, "Top o' the mornin' to ya, laddie!" with an over-embellished Irish accent.

You needn't wait for the child to make eye contact or seek you out first, because the odds are against the neediest children taking those steps. That's why you're the professional adult: You'll step out on that limb first.

Get specific. Learn the children's names and use them frequently. Hearing your name makes you feel special, like the other person really knows and cares about you. (This works for our neighborhood grocery store clerk, who says, "Thank you for coming in today, Mr. Griswold," so you return to that store even though the behemoth chain three blocks down might save you some hard-earned ducats.) Ask them about their families, their pets, their interests . . . and if all else fails, ask a random question like, "Hey Alonna, which do you suppose grows faster: dandelions or crocuses?" You might have to explain what a crocus is, but that's also part of the experience.

Use compliments. Compliment anything and everything, using specific language. This coming Monday, pick the most homely looking little girl in your school and tell her she's got the most beautiful smile this morning. Then, for a week, call her "beautiful" every time you see her. Watch her beam and sparkle before Friday's lunch.

Commit to it. Brother, can you spare seven seconds? Chances are you can. Are you willing to? Dedicate yourself to making a positive difference every day. Commit to lighting a child up every morning. Devote the energy to being a beacon in a child's life. Set aside seven seconds and watch it work.

It only takes seven seconds to make a child's day.

What might be the implications of not using those seven seconds for that purpose?

Get Out of That Chair!

Management By Walking Around (MWA). Walkthroughs. Touring the castle. Learning Walks. Doing the rounds. Call it what you will, *proactive supervision* is all the rage in education circles for a good reason: It works!

No information gleaned from textbooks, no knowledge obtained through years of experience, and no data compiled from test scores can carry nearly the weight as the awareness of what is going on in your own building right here, right now. The benefits of pedometer-busting classroom tours are many and immediate, and they dictate that the process be a priority of every effective principal's day.

Walkthroughs, as many of us commonly refer to the process of gathering information as we actively walk through classrooms, are the ultimate educational leadership tool. Of course the walkthrough process contains potential flaws, but with awareness you can relegate those roadblocks to mere obstacles.

Walkthroughs Answer Many Questions

When employed properly, walkthroughs provide principals a clear picture of the state of learning in their schools, and many peripheral benefits too. Walkthroughs can answer—directly and indirectly—many questions about which effective principals should be fully informed.

What is the current status of the teaching and learning in your school? This seems obvious, but there are still principals out there who wait until the formal teacher evaluation period to monitor instruction in their schools. Those are the same principals who wait until the test scores arrive to determine the amount of student learning taking place. *Don't be those principals!* Inspect what you expect. When you walk into a classroom, you can immediately determine the rates of student engagement, observe the instructional strategies employed by the teacher, and see the results of those things in the students' work. And you know what's going on, which is the most important information you can have as the building leader.

How can the principal build relationships with staff and students? Too often, the students we principals know best are the ones who frequent our offices for disciplinary reasons. In addition, it can be difficult to schedule meetings with teachers because their preparation time is so valuable and we are so busy with administrative work. But it's time to turn those realities on their ears. Walking in and out of classrooms provides us time to observe the children in their element: reading, working, learning. Sashaying through the hallway gives us an informal locale for impromptu conversations with staff members. Meandering from table to table within a classroom lets us get to know the children as students, ask about their work, and become an integral part of the educational experience. Sauntering from room to room grants our teachers the chance to engage in quick, non-curriculum-threatening dialogue. And for all those reasons, walkthroughs provide common experiences about which teachers and principals can relate.

How can the principal provide immediate and frequent feedback to teachers? The formal evaluation process, which is valuable in its own right, is often an isolated piece of a very intricate puzzle. Any given teacher teaches roughly six lessons a day for 180 days a year; that's roughly 1,080 lessons in a school year. Is a series of two or three hour-long observations followed by structured conversation the most appropriate and complete manner in which to assess the instructor's skills and abilities, to strengthen professional practice, and to deliver useful and targeted feedback? Engaging in walkthroughs more frequently allows you, as the principal, to share immediate feedback with teachers. As part of the walkthrough process, leave behind a written note with some observations, compliments, and questions. Make it a point to meet with the teacher briefly after class or en route to the staff room to discuss an element of the lesson. Use a handheld camera to videotape yourself posing questions or offering comments and e-mail a copy directly to the teacher. Whatever feedback format you choose, the point is to let the teacher know what you observed and how you interpreted it. Nothing is more nerve-wracking than a principal's visitation with no follow-up. It leads to confusion and consternation. A simple little note clarifies any situation, or, at the very least, invites more discourse.

Why does Martin always get sent to the office? Oh, we all have students who are repeat offenders and never seem to be able to keep their noses clean for more than 30 seconds. But how often do we see them in their classrooms, working and learning and firing spitballs among their peers? Might there be a reason Martin is sent out of Mrs. Cordell's class every morning at the same time? Could it be that when he's asked to work independently at a center, for example, he gets so frustrated that he misbehaves to avoid work? Whatever the circumstance, your understanding increases as you gain information. You might even choose to sit with Martin and help him work, all the while emphasizing proper behaviors and work habits. The benefits could extend beyond the immediate results. You might find that you like helping and talking to Martin. Martin might like it, too. The teacher might like it. The kid Martin usually needles with his pencil might like it. And Martin might just become a bit more motivated to focus on making better choices. If not, by spending time in Martin's classroom you certainly have gained a better understanding of his experiences, and that will help you when you meet with his parents and the counselor to determine a behavior plan.

How can I possibly get myself out of the office long enough to do this? *Aha!* That is the question that plagues many well-intentioned, competent principals. With all the demands made by the central office, parent groups, faculty, student supervision, piles of e-mails and paperwork, formal evaluations, barrages of phone calls, and discipline, what time is left over for walkthroughs? I propose that question is backwards. The better question to ask is this: What time do you prioritize for walkthroughs, and how willing are you to let your instructional leadership demands dictate your time management strategy? I know we all have deadlines, emergencies happen, and some things—such as testing, evaluations, and student supervision—can only happen during the school day, but can't the majority of the remaining tasks wait until after school? You cannot conduct walkthroughs after school, but you can answer e-mails. You cannot meander or sashay through classrooms before school, but you can sift through the mounds of paperwork. Do yourself, your staff, and, most important, your students, a gigantic favor: Make the walkthrough process a priority, and follow that calling with consistency and earnest. The benefits will astound you.

The National Association of Elementary School Principals' (NAESP) third standard for effective school leadership reads:

"Effective leaders demand content and instruction that ensure student achievement of agreed-upon academic standards."

What better way to monitor with precision than to engage in frequent, feedback-laden, fervent, faithful, forthcoming, and frankly, fun walkthroughs?

Who's Doing the Work Here, Anyway?

Picture this in your mind's eye: You're at school. It's nearing dismissal time, and your pulse is racing. Why? Because you're standing by the exit doors in Wing C, bracing yourself for a stampede rivaled only by the running of the bulls in Pamplona—the massive, screaming exodus of children from your school.

R-r-r-r-ing! Off goes the bell, and out go the children. A wild swarm of excitement, accompanied by loud voices and boisterous behavior, engulfs the entire scene. Kids are smiling, laughing, jumping, cartwheeling, yelling, and chicken-dancing. And as soon as it starts, it's over (or so we hope).

But it's not over. There's something behind the students. Ahoy! Look there! What is it? Bedraggled, harried, and slumped over, the shuffling form of a classroom teacher casts a new shadow on the doorway. It's been a long, tiring, wearisome, exhausting day.

What's wrong with this picture? Why are the kids catapulting themselves into the great big world while the teachers are dragging themselves down the dimly-lit hallway?

What Are We Working On?

There's no disputing that teachers, as a collective mass, are a hardworking bunch. Unless you buy into the uninformed prattle that bemoans educators' short workday and workyear, you'll likely rank teachers among the hardest working (and least-compensated) professionals in our solar system.

And, in your school, you have some teachers who seem to work doubly hard. Tireless and dedicated, these teachers may be the first to turn on the coffee machine in the morning and the last to unplug the laminator in the evening. In between, they're a blur streaking between the staff workroom to the copy machine to the classroom to a colleague's classroom upstairs to the cafeteria and back to the staff workroom. There's never enough time for these folks to finish all the work they've set out to accomplish. And they do this all with the best of intentions and a deep commitment to their students.

But in the final appraisal, the students in these teachers' classrooms may not be making significant strides. Despite all the hours, toil, blood, glue, and sweat their teachers have poured into their work, the student achievement rates aren't climbing. What gives? How can we explain this lack of correlation?

Discipline, Courage, and Focus

I'll just spit this out there: Many of us are spending a *tremendous* amount of time and a *monumental* amount of energy in low-yield practices. We're not getting the bang for our buck.

Which suggests three questions:

1. Do we have the courage to say NO to traditions and accepted practice? Some things we just do because that's what we've always done. This is true of any school—the spelling lessons, the assemblies, the dress code, the homework policy, the lunch-line routine, the thematic units, the holiday parade, the bulletin board decorations, the report-card comments. You name it. We've all experienced tradition.

Many traditions are worth keeping to build upon the school's culture, but some just don't come clean in the wash. Some of our practices don't necessarily lead to any student growth along any grade-level standard at any time on any planet. Just because, "that's the way we've done it here for generations," doesn't mean, "that's what leads to student growth." Can we say no?

2. Do we have the discipline to take things OFF our teachers' plates? (We certainly *add* to their plates enough, don't we?) Think about it: Do you have any new district initiatives this year? Any new textbook adoptions? Has anyone attended a new training and come back gung-ho to change the way we all do business? Any remediation funding? School choice? Paperwork for a grant? Scheduling adaptations? New protocols for data analysis?

It's easy for a principal to say, "Oh, this new approach to math problem-solving will solve all of our problem-solving problems," and it might well be true. However, what the teachers hear is, "Here's another 40-minute activity you'll need to squeeze in three times a week on top of everything else you already do. What are you making that face for? And wait, don't leave yet, we also have a new traveling science lab! Oy! Where are you going?"

A good rule for adoptions and initiatives has two tines, like a fruit fork: A) Ignore it; rather, get good at what you already do and stave off the mad rush to do "the next best thing" until you've mastered the current focus, or B) If choice A isn't possible because of a district-level, state, federal, or legal mandate, then agree to find *two* things to remove from the teachers' plates and wipe them into the disposal. You can't keep piling clothes into the closet unless you're willing to empty off a couple of hangers first, so make room.

3. Do we understand the formula for focus? News flash: Education isn't rocket science. There are formulas for rocket science. There is no formula for the education of children. However, if there were a formula, it would look like this: $E = wt2c$, where E is "education" and $wt2c$ is the "written, taught, and tested curriculum."

The Spokane Public Schools in the state of Washington, along with many other school districts, has made a living embracing this simple concept: If we assess our students beforehand, create a common curriculum based upon what the students *need* to have, teach that curriculum and fill in what the students *don't* have, and then assess the students again to be sure they got it, we will probably have good results. There will be learning. Like rocket science. It's time that we, as educators, evaluate everything that we do in our classrooms. We need to align every decision, every book, every lesson, every instructional strategy, and every assessment with our stated and agreed-upon grade-level standards. Follow the formula.

Develop the courage to say NO to traditions that don't align. Strengthen the discipline to remove the disconnected elements from our teachers' plates. Hone the focus on the formula for, well, *focus*. Let's eliminate the clutter. Remove the extraneous matter. Confiscate the wayward influences. Amputate the superfluous and incongruous *stuff*.

Let's work hard, and encourage our teachers to work hard. But only on the high-yield activities that directly align with grade-level standards. Then, in the end, it can be our teachers who skip around after the bell rings and the students can drag themselves home, exhausted after a hard day of working their brains.

Four Things You Must Do in the New Year

What follows was originally written right around New Year's Day, so it's most apropos during that time of year. However, the big picture is just as relevant in March, July, or November, because we're in charge of when we want a fresh start, not our calendars.

If you look outside, you can see it's January. January is easy to identify since it's frosty, people are wearing scarves, and our garbage cans are cluttered with broken snow shovels, old socks, tinsel, and the shiny boxes in which our New Year's Resolutions arrived.

Unfortunately, there are no warning labels on those boxes, and many of us open them whimsically and attack the contents with a reckless abandon that might make Bob, the rabid workout trainer from The Biggest Loser, blush in hesitation.

This essay is here to help you, dear readers, as you strive to be a better you. As we flip our calendars to reveal there is no next page, we also flip over that proverbial new leaf. We spend a few minutes, between sips of eggnog and bites of peanut brittle, to evaluate our lives and to determine a couple of steps that will help us get fit, get more in touch with ourselves, get happy, get peace, or get lost. And we write down those goals in the form of New Year's Resolutions.

Why? Why do we do this? Good questions. We do this because we know, deep down, that self-improvement is a critical piece of fulfillment and happiness. Are we successful at it? Another good question, to which I reply: Do you realize that the top items sold on eBay during the month of February every year are pieces of exercise equipment?[1]

We set for ourselves unreasonable, unrealistic, and unrealizable goals. We go whole-hog at that treadmill for a couple of weeks, 45 minutes a day on the hilly course, then we inadvertently hang that one shirt over the handles, followed by a box or two that will just sit on the tread temporarily. We'll get to the workouts again soon, we say. But the change in our routines was too immediate, too dramatic, too shocking to our systems. Pretty soon the treadmill is just another computerized closet. What was supposed to be a surge into healthiness has become a sashay into clutterdom.

For this New Year, let's tone it down just a little bit. Let's promise ourselves we won't overdo it with pledges we can't keep. Let's make a few subtle shifts in our attitudes that can pay substantial dividends in our daily routines. We're educators, right? Let's educate ourselves.

Four Pledges We Can Keep

1. Do everything else on this list. A professional trainer once gave me this advice: "Only give your audience three big ideas in a presentation. Any more than that and they become fuddled." That seems sane to me, so I'll follow the guideline. But, since in previous essays I've offered the "Three Golden Rules" and "My Three Favorite Things," I figured it was time to use a new numeral, so I've added a phony fourth. Let's proceed with the (rest of the) list.

2. Be the duck. When the parents start a-yellin' and the students start a-fightin', when the teachers start a-screamin' and the fish just aren't a-bitin', let it be. We can't make everyone happy all the time, and some things just don't go as planned. We can't control all things that happen, but we can control how we respond to them. So, when it becomes crazy, let it roll off your back. Get over it. Focus on what's important. Keep your

---

[1]This is not true, but it's believable fiction. I have no idea about eBay's sales, but I can tell you I know a lot of people that bought and scrap-heaped their exercise equipment in short order because they lacked the self-discipline and motivation to make it happen.

eyes and mind on the 595 reasons that all is good in your building, not the five that are crummy. Waxy, water-repellent layers on a duck's feathers keep the water rolling off. Develop your own waxy layers, smile, and move on to the next challenge.

3. Take time for you. Before the day. During the day. After the day. Anytime. Have you noticed that, as the building principal, everyone expects you to be everything to everyone? That's a tall order, and despite the fact that it's irrational, it really won't change. *Principal* is synonymous with *superhero*. However, whether you're Wonder Woman or Mr. Incredible, you're no good to anyone else if you're not good to yourself. So pause every once in awhile to put life in perspective. Stay hydrated. Exercise. Smile. Read. Listen to music. Don't neglect your duties, but set aside a minute or two here and there to stop and smell the weeds. You never know what flowers might be blooming nearby.

4. Find the positive in every negative. I know, you've heard that before, but it's too difficult to practice. Here's an idea: Make a list of all the people and things that irritate you. Then write ten compliments you could pay those people, ten aspects of those individuals that you respect, admire, or like; and ten ways that you can make those relationships and thoughts more positive and productive. Look at those lists frequently, or even daily. The more you read them, the more you'll believe them. The more you believe them, the more you'll live them. Pretty soon those irritants can be sources of tremendous positive energy in your life. That works for schedules, colleagues, parents, children, pencil sharpeners, and car batteries, among other things.

Each of the four (ha!) suggestions on this list is not too time-consuming. And each is simple to embrace. If it helps you to make them a reality, write the three ideas at the bottom of every page on your new calendar. That's right, every page. Then:

- Make a tally-mark each time you shrug off an angry parent's insult or an idea gone wrong.
- Draw stars for each time you push your metaphorical *pause* button and place yourself at the bottom of the totem pole. (Remember, most tribes depicted the highest-ranking member at the base of the totem pole!)

◆ Write your list of nuisances (with positive viewpoints) on a 3 × 5 card and keep it in your pocket for handy reference.

Whatever it takes, help yourself to make this new year the one in which you believed in yourself, and you began to always strive to be a better you.

REFLECTION QUESTIONS

In Part III, you awoke to the reality that you're in charge of your approach and attitude, no matter what happens during the day. How will this impact your daily grind? Use the following questions to guide your thinking about the ideas presented in Part III and the strategies you'll employ to implement them to motivate yourself or others. Then make it happen.

1. The Latin phrase *supera diem* means "survive the day." How does this compare/contrast with the more commonly known phrase *carpe diem*, which means "seize the day"? How might you use *supera diem* to keep yourself or others motivated to sail in rough seas?
2. Think about the single greatest day in your life. Feel the euphoria surrounding the events that provided you such joy. Revel in it. Now: How can you breathe life into the everyday, mundane routines to make them become the ecstatic, amazing, fun-filled events that we both remember fondly and look forward to earnestly?
3. Education is stressful, I've been told. What fun events do you lead? What strategies can you implement to raise the fun-meter in the people you lead or influence? What challenges can you issue to your colleagues? What goals for fun can you set for yourself?
4. Answer the question, "Who's your Joey Amalfitano?" Then, perhaps more importantly, what intentional steps will you take to ensure that you've got repeated access to your Joey Amalfitano whenever you need him/it to keep you motivated?

5. Think of something that (or someone who) let you down recently. Why did it affect you the way that it did? Now consider it from another angle. What lesson can you learn from this event? What benefits did it afford you? They might be hidden, so dig deep. What's the silver lining in this cloud?

6. When you have a project you're working on, how can you ensure that you remain focused on the task at hand? Do you have clearly identified priorities at work? Do you stay true to them? If so, carry on. If not, list the actions/behaviors/habits that are interfering with your productivity and attention, and *stop it*! Make a pledge to eliminate the distractions and share it with a critical friend or trusted colleague.

7. Have you ever caught yourself thinking (or, heaven forbid, saying aloud), "Oh, that would never work," or "That's all we can expect from him," or "You've set that goal too high," or other negative thoughts? What might lead you to install those ceilings on people, dreams, or goals? What steps can you take to eliminate those ceilings and to reinstall the visions of excellence?

8. Educators often lament their lack of energy at the end of the day, especially in contrast to their students' boundless exuberance. Are there actions that you take right now that perhaps the students should be taking themselves? How can you help to shift the onus of responsibility and the initiative back to the learners? What will you do to motivate others to do likewise?

9. Do you find yourself taking professional attacks personally? Why or why not? Think of the last time someone questioned your professionalism, a decision you made, or an action you took. How did you respond to it? How might you reframe that interaction in a way that left you coolly dispassionate and open to the professional growth that accompanies honest criticism (even if it's inaccurate)?

PART IV

The Principalship

The school principal is the single most influential individual playing in the game of education today. Which other position maintains leverage over the minutiae in a schoolhouse on a daily basis—the very place where students spend an inordinate amount of their waking hours through age 18—and has a voice in the creation of curriculum, assessments, and initiatives that is heard at the district and state offices of education? The school principal performs the most significant role of any member of the educational community, buffering teachers from wild demands from officials several degrees removed from the reality of schooling, creating a culture of learning in a building that demands no less than excellence, and ensuring that every teacher upholds the belief that every child who crosses the classroom threshold has an opportunity for a world-class education.

This is the idealist's version of the principalship and its influence. It was mine before I was chosen to lead a school for the first time. And, after spending a decade in the principal's office, it's still the mindset that directs my professional endeavors. I'll stand behind that claim.

Ultimately, what is the mission we're called to lead? Why do we accept the tour of duty as school principals? We're in charge of a future. We're in control of a dream. We're responsible for results.

Richard Allington (2007), former president of the International Reading Association, once came to my school to speak to the staff about instructional excellence. He spoke about literacy development and our obligation to strengthen every child's reading and writing abilities. That, however, wasn't the end unto itself. Rather, those literacy skills offered simply the foundations of a strong education. And that, fellow principals, leads us to the goal he explained in *Schools That Work*:

> We need schools that educate children—not schools that simply sort children into worker groups. We need schools that help children exceed their destiny—schools where all children are successful, not just the lucky ones who find schooling easy. We need schools that develop in all children the knowledge, skills, and attitudes that have historically been reserved for a few. (p. 2)

But, of course, it's not always as easy to implement as it is to shout from the mountaintops. The principalship is a bizarre blend of lunacy and enlightenment. Tumult and chaos perch on a principal's shoulder and duke it out with pride and bliss, and each round could be decided by a series of uppercuts and cheap shots. Ronald Wolk, the founder of *Education Week*, shared a description of the reality of the principalship that we principals might find amusingly familiar (from his 2011 book, *Wasting Minds*):

> Anyone who shadows the principal of a large urban high school for a day soon discovers that the "principal instructional leader" (like teachers) lives in real time, with little opportunity for planning or reflection and almost no time for instruction or collaboration with colleagues. In large schools, the principal, often with a squawking walkie-talkie in hand, patrols the halls herding students to class, peering into classrooms, and handling a variety of crises. As with teachers, universities' preparation programs do not prepare principals for the real world of schools and are often irrelevant to the reality the principal will face. (p. 71)

This is why I often advocate for more and stronger mentorship programs for school leaders. Every principal, and not just the rookies or those struggling with the role, could benefit from a consistent mentoring influence. I was fortunate to have some fantastic role models guiding me through the first few years of my administrative career, and I've continued to seek out trusted colleagues to keep me balanced, to keep me up-to-date, and to keep me sane. And that's no easy job.

The principalship is complicated. It's busy. It's hectic, unpredictable, fast-paced, menacing, callous, tempestuous, and amazing. Thrilling. Grand. Rewarding. Meaningful. Fun.

Sure, the challenges sometimes seem to dominate the landscape, as we're fighting for our professional lives every time the newspaper runs our schools' test scores. The accountability for results pushes all of us to the brink, but the knowledge that we make a real difference—beyond test scores, in crazy things like attitudes, appreciation for learning, zest for life, self-confidence, and other "intangibles"—keeps us roaring back for more.

How do we accomplish our goals, when we're faced with antagonism, conflict, a constant stream of problems to solve, tempers, and a string of demands that, when stacked up, would reach the moon? We stay true to the mission, as you'll read in "Mentoring and the Three Golden Rules." We do it together, as I'll share in "T2—Togetherness and Teamwork." Finally, we focus on the things we can, indeed, affect, as you'll note in the essays that comprise Part IV. Go get 'em, principals!

Delegate and Prioritize Your Way to Effective Leadership

The principalship is a difficult job. Anyone who tells you otherwise works at the golf course.

Think for a moment about the hundreds of interactions we have over the course of a week, the thousands over a month, or the hundreds of thousands over a year. Consider the swarms of individual faces that come calling with requests, questions, comments, ideas, and complaints. Ponder the reams of paperwork that we are expected to complete by unforgiving deadlines. Contemplate the decisions, both immediate and long-term—combining simple tasks and complex consequences—that we make on the job.

Now breathe.

Effective principals engage in two extremely worthwhile activities with high degrees of success: prioritization and delegation. If we cannot effectively prioritize time and energy, and if we cannot delegate certain tasks and decisions, then we will find ourselves dangling at the end of a very short rope over a frothing sea of sharks, piranhas, and other scary creatures (like talk-radio personalities).

Delegation

What's the big deal about delegating? Heavens, our jobs are hectic, non-stop, demanding, roller-coasters with a shot of WD-40. Delegation is a must. It's a strategy that bullies, bookies, the mafia, and male lions have utilized for generations. However, they may not be our role models, so we're left to explore and learn the art of delegation on our own.

Release control. Even though many people think of the principal as the CEO (Chief Everything Officer) of the school, recent studies show it actually benefits everyone on campus if others are allowed to make decisions. If too much control is concentrated in one person, the school environment actually loses balance. Empower others. If you're a power monger, start by sharing small decisions that don't really matter. Then, as others in the school community build capacity and earn the trust of the troops, let them become more involved in the real decisions of the school. You'll be amazed at how relieved you feel, and how powerful the school becomes.

Reject the monkey. In Kenneth Blanchard's ridiculously simple analogy, *The One-Minute Manager Meets the Monkey,* a "monkey" represents the responsibility to achieve a task. Every time your teachers ask you to do something, or suggest an idea, and you respond, "I'll check into that and get back to you," you've allowed their monkey to leap off their back and onto yours. Then you have to make the next move, make the follow-up phone call, or plan the next meeting. Meanwhile, they're sipping gin at the Cask 'n Flagon and comparing hairdos. Instead, fire right back. Say, "Why don't you call so-and-so and find out how much that will cost, then get back to me?" Your monkey shield will protect you from absorbing a dozen extra tasks, and will also free you up to handle the important stuff.

Consider the task. Does the request in question really fall under your jurisdiction? What could you be doing instead? Could this be someone else's responsibility? If so, snap out of it and let the right person do the job. Yes, it sends a strong signal about your dedication if you are willing to do *anything* to help the school, but it also raises a red flag about a potential weakness if you try to do everything yourself. It's your job to make sure everything is done, done right, and done on time. So make sure the right people are on the case.

Prioritization

When it comes to prioritization, we make a slight shift in urgency. Rather than asking, *"What could I be doing?"* we ask ourselves instead, *"What **should** I be doing?"* That query probes to the deepest, darkest part of our inner selves, to the cockles of our heart. It might even get us below the cockles, in the sub-cockle area. There we will find the driving force that generates all our professional actions, dreams, goals, and motivation.

For most of us, that driving force is the continuous improvement of the educational process to benefit hordes of individual children, so they might one day become productive, healthy, contributing members of a greater society. Our actions indicate our priorities and preferences. They help us distinguish between what we deem important and what becomes a coat rack that stands in the corner collecting dust and umbrellas.

The question, *"What should I be doing?"* really requires a follow-up question: *"What do I **really** prioritize?"*

With student achievement, professional growth, and healthy development as cornerstones of our professional work, the issue of prioritization is of utmost importance. In a related essay, a clever author once wrote, "You cannot conduct walk-throughs after school, but you can answer e-mails" (Hall, 2011). That certainly speaks to the value and importance of setting aside chunks of time to engage in active instructional leadership. But what else is a whisper in your veins that sounds with every beat of your heart, rather than a Post-It note on the side of your desktop calendar? And how can you massage those priorities into your daily routines?

Quadrantize your work. Think of every decision you have to make and every task you have to complete according to its importance (its relationship to the achievement of your mission and goals) and its urgency (how quickly you must address it). Plot these items on Stephen Covey's (1989) Time-Management Matrix:

	Urgent	*Not Urgent*
Important	I. Quadrant of Necessity (MANAGE) ♦ Crisis ♦ Medical emergencies ♦ Pressing problems ♦ Deadline-driven projects ♦ Last-minute preparations for scheduled activities	II. Quadrant of Quality & Personal Leadership (FOCUS) ♦ Preparation/planning ♦ Prevention ♦ Values clarification ♦ Exercise ♦ Relationship-building ♦ True recreation/relaxation
Not Important	III. Quadrant of Deception (AVOID) ♦ Interruptions, some calls ♦ Some mail & reports ♦ Some meetings ♦ Many "pressing" matters ♦ Many popular activities	IV. Quadrant of Waste (AVOID) ♦ Trivia, busywork ♦ Junk mail ♦ Some phone messages/e-mail ♦ Time wasters ♦ Escape activities ♦ Viewing mindless TV shows

- ◆ Under high-importance, high-urgency (quadrant I) will be the fires and emergencies. You've got to stop everything to take care of these because they are matters of life and death.
- ◆ High-importance, low-urgency (quadrant II) will be visionary work, that which affects the school. You know it's necessary, but it's often left off your calendar because there's no dramatic urgency to get it done right now. In fact, you could just do it tomorrow.
- ◆ Low-importance, high-urgency (quadrant III) will be typical principal tasks with deadlines coming up. These are the items on your never ending to-do list.
- ◆ Low-importance, low-urgency (quadrant IV) will be things that get lost in the bottom of your in-box, those tasks that you really ought to distribute (read: delegate) to others.

As principals, we need to spend as much time in quadrant II as we can. We need to make it a point to do that every day. If we need help, we can always write those responsibilities into our daily schedules, like we do with all those darned quadrant III tasks.

Determine levels of controllability. What can you control? Are you working to solve problems beyond your realm of influence? Get back on track. Some characteristics of our profession are impossible to conquer. Reducing student mobility, dealing with contractual issues, battling district-supplied textbooks—you'd have a better chance of success if you were to play pick-up sticks with your pinky toe! Instead, focus your time and energy on teaching skills, professional development, behavioral management, teacher motivation, parent communication, and community awareness. Those beasts you can tame, so don't wrangle with the wild ones.

Imagine You're Invisible

Now that you're doing a better job of delegating and prioritizing, step back for a quiet moment. Imagine you are invisible. If you weren't present, how would your school suffer? Student discipline? Teacher discipline? Morale? Would your office chair blow away? If your school would have irreconcilable issues when you are stuck in Wichita during a snowstorm for a week, what would those issues be? Are they important ones? Or, would your school survive? Would it march forward resolutely emboldened to live its mission and to accomplish its goals?

Learn the art of delegation to empower others within the school community. Prioritize your own activities so your time is well spent and benefits the greatest number of individuals. Your school will thank you.

T2: Togetherness and Teamwork

Any good coach will tell you: "Sometimes you win, sometimes you lose, sometimes it rains." No, wait, that's from the movie *Bull Durham*, but it could be an accurate quote from a good coach.

What a *great* coach will tell you is that the *team* excelled. The coach made simple moves to allow the players to demonstrate their superiority, and together they got the job done.

Together: That's the Key Word

In today's schools, our challenges are more complex and intricate than ever before. This we know. Similarly, our knowledge about instruction, curriculum design, assessments, multiple learning styles, brain functioning, and school structures is complicated, comprehensive and, frankly, exhausting. It's too much for us to take on alone.

Thus, we see the importance of togetherness and teamwork. Quotes such as, "many hands make light work," "two heads are better than one," and, "it takes a village to raise a child" could not be more apropos than they are in today's schoolhouses. We need each other.

There is a Kilimanjaro-sized mountain of research (that's right, 19,340 feet of it) supporting the creation of teams and the development of learning organizations to propel our schools forward in the pursuit of greatness, higher levels of learning, and increased efficiency. It's so clear and makes so much sense that any arguments to the contrary are moot and senseless. So let's move on. Together.

In education, the term most often associated with this work is the Professional Learning Community (PLC). Yours Truly defines a PLC as, "a collection of educators that always strives to perform at its ultimate potential, working together to learn, grow, and improve the professional practice of teaching in order to maximize student learning." An entire school community can comprise a PLC. Within that PLC, one of the first tasks is to establish teams, which makes sense even if you can't spell Kilimanjaro.

How Are Teams Established?

Teams come into being in one of two ways: They are either pre-ordained or ordained.

Preordained teams fall from the sky in perfect formation because that's the way they were meant to be, like grade-level teams (elementary), core subject teams (middle school), and departments (high school). There is a gravitational pull in every school that sorts teams into their primary spots. We call these "A Teams," and every staff member belongs to one.

Ordained teams are the ones that we as principals and school leaders establish. We see the need, we notice the relationships, we perceive the connections, and we put these folks together. These can be vertical teams, cross-department teams, or any of a million other varieties of compilations with common characteristics. We call these "B Teams," and every staff member should belong to one of these too. B Teams offer balance and perspective.

What Do We Do with Our Teams?

This may sound as if it's not well thought-out, but trust me as I provide four simple words of advice: Let them work together.

It's really that simple, too. Build time into the regular contracted schedule for teams—A Teams *and* B Teams—to meet and work collaboratively (defined by DuFour et al. in *Professional Learning Communities at Work* as, "a systematic process in which we work together interdependently to analyze and impact professional practice in order to improve our individual and collective results") and create repeated opportunities for true collaboration to occur.

There is a Grand Canyon-length list (that's right, 217 miles) of ways to establish built-in teacher collaboration time. That can be done by using substitutes, specialists, altered bell schedules, bus delays, common prep periods, stipends, or other carrots. We just need to be creative and talk with our peers about arranging it. As principals, it is our job to set it up.

Then we need to honor that time. Away with the impromptu staff meetings, the emergency pull-outs, the rearranged schedules, and the other interruptions that we "can't avoid." If collaboration is so necessary and helpful for teachers, let's treat it that way and *let them work together during that time*.

Setting Goals

Nothing is more frustrating than a team with no goals. Sports teams have it easy: their goal—winning the championship—is already clear. Are our goals in schools as easy to identify? The tricky part is that each individual teacher will have goals that sit upon three different hierarchical layers.

Schoolwide goals. These should be obvious, but they're not. It takes time to isolate and elucidate an all-systems goal. The questions we ask of the staff during the process should include

- ♦ What is non-negotiable to us?
- ♦ What will we do no matter what?
- ♦ What do we expect to accomplish through our work?
- ♦ What is our "Hedgehog Concept"? (Jim Collins, in *Good to Great*, defines this as the clarity and drive with which the organization will produce long-term results.)

A Team and B Team goals. These (preordained and ordained) teams have their own challenges, their own focal points, and their own interests. Their goals, while aligning with the schoolwide, hedgehog-concept goal, will likewise have a particular slant. This is good, and this is where the real action is. If the teams have focus and clarity of vision, they can move mountains. It is most helpful if these goals coordinate with the schoolwide goals.

Individual goals. As unique and special human beings, every member of the teaching staff brings different experiences, preferences, training, strengths, weaknesses, and vices to the job. It is our responsibility to work with each individual to connect the dots between the schoolwide goal, the team goals, and the needs of that individual to belong, improve, and perform within those frameworks. So individuals have their own, duly related goals. Inasmuch as it is possible, the most meaningful individual goals will speak to the individual teacher's contributions to the team goals and or the schoolwide goals. This will, in turn, bring continuity and focus to our work.

Fluid Goals

In reference to goals, we have all heard the acronym SMART—Specific, Measurable, Attainable, Results-oriented, and Timebound. We know what the terms mean, but the one that frequently muddles our goal-setting process is the T: timebound.

In the school setting, our mindset is to assign designated lengths of time to goals—often a full ten-month school year. The problem there is that, though tidy for record-keeping purposes, rarely is there a goal that requires precisely ten months of development, work, support, tinkering, evaluating, and revamping to be successfully achieved.

Effective goals are unique, fluid, flexible, and shifting. If an A Team only needs to drill deeply into problem-solving strategies for six weeks to complement the schoolwide "Math Hub" goal, then *let them work together* for six weeks, analyze their results, and extend or select a new goal. There are more goals buried in the nether lands of poor time-framing than there are bodies adorned with concrete boots at the bottom of Lake Tahoe (and that is quite a few, according to local legends).

The true issue is the development of individuals, teams, and teaching staffs to better meet the needs of our students. We, as school leaders, can demonstrate that we share those goals, and that we have the flexibility and with-it-ness to allow for teams to chart their own course and navigate their own waters, even if they flow like the Sebaskachu River in central Labrador, which meanders like crazy but follows one undeniable hedgehog concept: gravity.

Then let them work *together.*

The Matter of Mentoring

I read a startling statistic the other day about the future of school administration: In the next five years, nearly 50 percent of our nation's public school administrators will retire, leaving quite a void in one of the most critical leadership roles in American society. The folks who will fill those positions are likely to share characteristics I had a lifetime ago: young, relatively inexperienced, thin-necked, and totally, blissfully, unequivocally unprepared for the avalanche we call the principalship.

New principals have no idea what they're about to encounter when they walk from their newly decorated parking spots into the offices of their new schools. This is not their districts' fault for hiring incompetent leaders, nor does the blame sit on the shoulders of their internship supervisors, their university professors, the state licensing board, or their own selves for accepting the positions. The principalship is simply a beast that cannot be understood until one has wrangled with it.

Those statements speak not to new principals' character, leadership style, personality, knowledge, integrity, intelligence, communication abilities, or genetic makeup. Rather, they are simple observations about preparation, and they send sparks flying about the importance of providing quality mentorship programs for our rookie administrators.

Our newbie leaders are in desperate need of someone to guide them, listen to them, offer advice, encourage them, and reassure them that all the strange events that happen in and around the principal's office are, in fact, normal, and that there are reasonable ways to handle every bizarre and unorthodox circumstance.

You cannot possibly prepare yourself to simultaneously receive a phone call from the superintendent requesting a copy of a lost report, settle a dispute between two students engaged in a fistfight, pacify a rabid parent, locate a teacher who did not report to collect her students from the library, drink enough water to maintain adequate levels of hydration, and raise test scores significantly until you have found yourself in such a position.

Having participated in, and later served as a coach and trainer for, the National Association of Elementary School Principals' National Principal Mentor Certification Program, I've seen all of the research and witnessed firsthand dozens of examples of how important having a loyal, supportive, present mentor can be. Every new principal should have one, like a spare change of clothes hanging on the office door and a toothbrush.

In the absence of a formal mentor, however, we have self-help books. By definition, however, those preclude mentorships. Jim Collins, in *Good to Great*, mentions several times that the grooming of future leaders helped ease transitions between CEOs for organizations that built substantial, long-term success. Leadership is generally noted as a requirement for school improvement and a requisite for increasing student achievement, but there is very little literature outlining the severe need for the development of leadership capacity at the school level.

Three Golden Rules

Alas, lacking that connection with an effective mentor, here is a triad of guidelines I affectionately refer to as the Three Golden Rules (first published, in all places, in my 2004 book, *The First-Year Principal*). I suggest that all principals, particularly those new to the profession who have yet to establish their niche and position within the school community, refer to them in the significant likelihood that you are expected to make a decision. If ever in doubt, in a bind, or overwhelmed, follow these rules to make each and every decision:

Stay true to the shared vision. We principals make literally hundreds of decisions in a typical week, and it's important to understand the motivation within ourselves that guides our decision-making process. Every decision, every mandate, every statement, every prioritized list, and every comment must be justifiable to anybody and everybody involved. If the school has a clear, established, and embraced vision, put the decision in question up to this standard: Is this aligned with our shared vision? If your school has not yet ironed out an agreed-upon vision, a safe support vehicle might be the answer to this question: Is this in the best interest of the school as a whole, or in the best interest of our students? If you can show a strong relationship between the decision and the school's vision, you can still justify decisions that go dreadfully wrong and it's unlikely that anyone will question your motives.

Be aware of the goings-on. Information is a premium, and there is truly no substitute for knowing the routines, characteristics, idiosyncrasies, and practices that populate your school community. As the leader, it is your responsibility, obligation, and duty to know the behaviors of the humans under your care, the schedules followed by students and staff, the interactions and relationships on board, the contents of every bulletin board, the teaching styles and discipline procedures of every teacher, and any special circumstance that might set today apart from the rest of your lives. So use those eyes and ears for all they're worth—listen, observe, listen more, and continue to observe. Walk the grounds tirelessly. Get in every classroom, every day. Get to know the personnel as people, know what to expect, and identify if and when your expectations aren't being met. After all, if you do not know what is going on in your own school, how can you lead it to the shared vision?

Conduct yourself professionally. This seems like common sense, but it's amazing how many conversations, debates, interpersonal interactions, and working relationships are ruined beyond repair due to a lack of professionalism. As the school figurehead, you are fully expected to provide a beacon of righteousness, a pillar of appropriateness, and a steaming heap of polite political correctness. Though it's tempting to tell off a hostile parent drenched in irrationality, or to guffaw when a teacher complains about her scheduled bus duty, or to bellow at a student who is misbehaving again, the immediate explosions are destructive and demoralizing to everyone who later hears about the transmission. Rather than allowing yourself to be suckered into an argument, or saying what you really probably want to say, phrase your thoughts delicately with the big picture in mind. Take the proverbial high road and shun the frustrations, shackles, and irritations. Instead, be pleasant, maintain focus, listen, and then let it go. After all, you are a professional, so act like one.

If you can follow those three golden rules, you can survive the tsunami that we call the principalship, at least until some wayward administrator from a neighboring school throws you a rope and tugs you out of the grime.

Teacher Selection Counts: Six Steps to Hiring

If there were a job advertisement in the office, in the newspaper, or on the website of your local school, this might be how that sign would read:

> **HELP WANTED:** School teacher. Must work extraordinary hours for measly pay. Must shoulder great responsibility for student success. Must balance curricular requirements with individual student needs. Must follow orders lock-step, but also initiate creative efforts. Summers off (just kidding). Must remain emotionally detached, but psychologically connected at the same time. Must possess otherworldly sense of humor. Required characteristics: self-starter, reflective, sensitive, dedicated, data-savvy, street-smart. Acting and dancing experience preferred.

As principals, there is an enormous amount of pressure on us to staff our buildings with strong, effective, intelligent people. We feel the push to hire the best person and to simultaneously make the right fit *and* appease local political forces (district offices, teachers' associations, parent groups, neighborhood councils, the current teaching staffs, and so on). Doing that is not as easy as one might think.

Teacher Quality Is the #1 Determinant of Student Success

Consider the words of experts:

Great teaching matters: Bob Marzano, author of *What Works in Schools,* says, "It is clear that effective teachers have a profound influence on student achievement" (2003).

Great teaching makes a difference: Charlotte Danielson, author of *Enhancing Professional Practice: A Framework for*

Teaching, tells us, "High-level learning by students requires high-level instruction by their teachers" (2007).

Great teaching is the key: Mike Schmoker, author of *Results Now: How We Can Achieve Unprecedented Improvements in Teaching and Learning,* claims, "The single greatest determinant of learning is not socioeconomic factors or funding levels. It is instruction" (2006).

How Do We Get Great Teaching?

First, we can train and build our current teachers' capacity for success through effective use of coaching, professional development opportunities, differentiated supervision practices, targeted feedback, and hot, caffeinated beverages.

Second, and this is the topic of the essay *du jour,* we can hire great teachers. And if you're a principal who has ever had to fill a teaching vacancy, you know how hard that is: Hard as a coffin nail.

It's difficult to do what leadership expert Jim Collins (*Good to Great* and *Built to Last*) suggests is necessary: Get the right people on the bus, and put them in the right seats (2001). Fortunately, we have a set of guidelines for you to follow the next time you're faced with a spot on your teaching roster with no name next to it.

Six Steps to Hiring

Recruit. Public relations is not someone else's job. Go find the great people, and encourage them to apply. Talk to your colleagues about potential candidates. Put a school brochure on the billboard in the local university's school of education building. Rent a biplane that trails a banner with your school's phone number on it. Get the word out that your fantastic school needs another fantastic team member.

Scour. When the applications and résumés are in, go through them with a fine-toothed comb. Know what you're looking for, and look for it. If you need some fresh ideas, search for someone educated in another state. If you need an infusion of spirit and attitude, check personal e-mail addresses. There's probably a *wickedsillyteachaholic@wherever.com* in there somewhere! Don't fall victim to the blasé, mind-numbing, page-turning exercises that are so enticing. Scour.

And, while you are scouring, if writing skills are important to you (aren't they?), don't even look twice at those résumés that include misspelled words, bad spacing, inconsistent fonts, and so on. Pitch them! Throw them away! If the person didn't take the time to represent himself in a glowingly positive light in that all-too-critical first-impression document, he probably won't in the back-to-school letter to the parents either, and almost certainly won't over the long course of a career. Ugh! Save yourself!

And when the candidates come in for an interview, don't hesitate to ask them to do some on-the-spot writing. You will learn whether that meticulous résumé was a carefully proofed façade *or* if the applicant can, indeed, string together a few words.

Collaborate. Hiring isn't something the principal should ever do solo. Invite the key players in the position to participate in screening papers, describing desirable traits, and interviewing. This isn't to absolve you of any culpability if the person turns out sour. Instead, it provides wider perspectives to help ensure you're selecting the right person.

Elicit. During the interview, elicit the information you really need. Keep in mind what soft skills (qualities like work ethic, resourcefulness, personality) and hard skills (technical expertise, knowledge, experience) you require in this position. Craft and ask the questions that will elicit that information. Look for the candidate's true colors peeking through the veil of finely crafted answers—really take this time to figure out who this person really is. I like to ask candidates, "What's so great about you that would make us interested in hiring you?" This gives us an idea if the person has confidence and can articulate what strengths and skills we'd be bringing into our school.

Scrutinize. When you have narrowed your field to a finalist (or two), dig into their closets and check out the skeletons. In the past, I've called candidates' sports coaches, church-group leaders, babysitters, and I even called one lady's mother! When I say, "Find out who they really are," I mean it. Call their references, even if they wrote glowing letters. If you hadn't noticed, it seems anyone can get a fabulous letter (or seven) in his or her file, and it's hard to determine how authentic they are. Go back and reread everything in the application folder—check handwriting, spelling, grades in appropriate coursework, trends in work patterns, and test scores. Pick up every bit of information you can.

Ensure. Eliminate vacillation. If you're not sure, the answer is always "no," and you start over. If you're sure, and I mean really, deeply, truly, assuredly positive that this is the right person at the right time for the right seat on your bus, then (and only then) go for it.

I can't stress that last point enough: Unless you're absolutely, positively, unequivocally, irreparably *certain* that this person is the right person, then remember the words of wisdom from Nancy Reagan: "Just say no." You can't expect to get the right people on the right seats of the bus if you simply pick, "the best person of the field of candidates we interviewed."

It's preferable to wait, fill the position with a qualified substitute, and keep searching. Wouldn't you rather have the right person for 163 days (and a sub for 17) than have to put up with the wrong person for 180 days and allow it to drain you of your resources, sanity, self-confidence, and your remaining non-gray hairs?

If you're not convinced, call your colleagues and ask them to tell you about a time that they hired the wrong person. Hear the still-simmering frustration in their voice. Feel the anguish in their expressions. Dab the tears from the corners of their eyes. Censor the profanity with which they describe this horrible series of events. Learn from their mistakes so you don't repeat them. Let's select teachers better. Our students deserve the best. The very best. The right people. In the right seats.

You drive the bus. It's up to *you!*

Turning Teacher Evaluations on Their Ears

Warning: Read this essay only if you are interested in improving your school by maximizing the skill, effectiveness, and self-reflective abilities of your teaching staff. Do not read any further if you are looking for shortcuts, ways to avoid work, paperwork reduction, passing the buck, or generational wealth; the strategies and philosophy herein will probably not help with those things.

Where I live in Idaho, turkey season opens April 15—darn near the time we're scrambling to finish our taxes, reveling in the beginning of the baseball season, and, of course, writing our teacher evaluations. I'm no hunter, but I pay taxes, love baseball, and set up camp in the principal's office that month. So it's an important, exciting time of year. And, like most principals, I often use adjectives such as "stressful," "overwhelming," and "hectic" to describe teacher-evaluation time.

For decades, teacher evaluations have thrown us all for a loop. The scheduling, the classroom observations, the discussions, the reports, the checklists, the double-check-to-make-sure-we-haven't-written-anything-that-the-union-folks-will-use-to-flay-us-later routines. It's an exhausting, demanding, tenuous adventure. Just ask our ulcers.

It's also a critical part of the most important work we do—teacher improvement.

The Most Successful Schools Do It

I'm sure you've all seen those widely circulated lists of characteristics shared by successful schools. One element finds its way onto every list I've seen. And if we were to prioritize, its impact on school improvement would be at the top, too. Of course we're talking about *teacher quality.*

When it comes to the issue of teacher quality, there is probably no more eloquent spokesperson than Kati Haycock of The Education Trust. The fact is, Haycock says, that running a string of five consecutive high-quality teachers in the elementary grades eliminates—not just reduces, but *eradicates*—the achievement gap.

Teacher quality matters immensely, which is why teacher evaluations matter immensely, too. One of its goals is to ensure quality control, making sure that every teacher is at least cutting the proverbial mustard. The other goal, however, is perhaps even more vital: Teacher evaluation time is our opportunity to boost school improvement by building teachers' capacity for success.

Increasing Effectiveness

Every school district has unique requirements for the teacher evaluation process. Some districts require a set number of formal observation periods. Some districts have a very specific protocol for principals to follow throughout this process. That doesn't mean that all principals follow those guidelines lockstep, however. I have worked with many different school districts and I have seen many different interpretations of the evaluation process in action.

You might not believe this (and you, as enlightened readers of this essay, certainly haven't done this), but some principals write teachers' evaluations without ever setting foot into those teachers' classrooms. Other principals cut-and-paste narratives and just change teachers' names, or submit nearly identical evaluations year after year. Some hand over the evaluations to the teachers so that they assess their performance themselves—without the principals ever adding any input. And some others ignore the realities of a teacher's performance, favoring instead to scribe innocuous pleasantries in order to pacify the teacher and prolong the "culture of nice," which leads nowhere but to bland instruction, mediocre education, and a stultified status quo.

Ugh. There is no capacity-building going on there.

But this idea is not out of anyone's reach. Regardless of the time we are required to spend in teachers' classrooms, regardless of the number and frequency of formal observations we must make, and regardless of the stipulations of the teachers' contracts and district protocol, one viewpoint remains startlingly clear: If we are going to improve our schools, we need to focus on the teachers.

Walkthroughs and Teacher Evaluations: Do They Mix?

If you're at all familiar with my work, you know how much I believe in the effectiveness of frequent, informal, classroom observations with specific feedback. We call those "walkthroughs."

Many districts and teachers' unions have addressed the walkthrough issue in one form or another. In some places, information gathered from walkthroughs is not allowed to enter evaluation documents. Instead, only data collected during formal, preannounced, scheduled, documented, signed-in-triplicate classroom observations can be used to provide summary feedback to teachers on their annual performance review. What kind of crazy perspective is *that?* I'm pretty sure there are children in the room 180 days a year, six hours a day, and I believe that every teacher's final evaluation should match their actual, yearly performance, regardless of how the data describing it were collected.

As principals, we have an opportunity (and obligation) to truly affect the quality of teaching that goes on in our buildings. Let's not waste it. If the final evaluation document is truly meant to be an accurate assessment of each teacher's performance over the course of the year, great. Let's collect as much information and data as we can to determine what the teacher did, how effective the action was, and what the implications are for future teaching. Here are some ideas:

Let's look at student data. Have you ever heard of a mechanic who isn't graded (and paid) on whether or not the car runs properly after working on it? Do we say the gardener is doing a great job planting trees if none of them grow and bear fruit? Teacher evaluations should include student output. That's the whole point of education, correct?

Let's look at how the teacher works as part of a collaborative team. Let's ask colleagues for input, let's talk with the students and their parents, and let's bring in the paraprofessionals that work with the teacher. Is there any reason to suspect that teaching is an isolated event? Should we assume that teaching takes place in the vacuum of that single lesson of the preplanned formal observation period? The rest of the year didn't really happen?

Let's look at performance throughout the year. The easiest and most authentic way to do this is to include walkthrough data. Informal observations. Pop-ins. Have a look at the teachers' performance in the trenches, in the wild, in the moment. Most importantly, since it is our job to ensure teacher growth, let's provide ongoing feedback, targeted support, and offer plenty of opportunities for each teacher to self-reflect. Let's work together. The final teacher evaluation document should neither be difficult to write nor contain surprises in content. It should be a step in the journey together, a summative assessment in a formative new world.

Capacity-Building as a Part of the Process

As school leaders, we are partners with our teachers in the educational process. We are coaches, mentors, supervisors, sages, battering rams, cheerleaders, facilitators, sounding boards, punching bags, hitching posts—you name it, we play the roles. If our teachers are strong and effective in what they do, our students benefit. If our teachers are weak and ineffective, the students suffer.

It makes sense to work with our teachers to ensure that they improve throughout the year. It makes sense to provide ongoing support and feedback to our teachers. It makes sense to observe them frequently and openly. It makes sense to view their work in the full context of the educational spectrum. And it makes sense to use the teacher evaluation document as a component of a capacity-building process.

We can't just *do* teacher evaluations because they're a requirement of our jobs. We need to *use* the evaluation process as a vehicle for change and improvement. We need to make it real, make it authentic, make it mean something.

If our energy isn't spent here, where are we spending it?

Confronting Concerns with Teacher Performance

Teaching is among the noblest of professions, that much is clear. Effective teachers are a commodity any society, school district, or neighborhood school would be wise to revere. We should heap praise on our best teachers, offer substantial financial remuneration, and carve giant statues of them to place in front of City Hall.

As principals, our responsibilities range far and wide, but right at the center is to inspire, motivate, and maximize the impact our teachers have on student learning. That is all well and good when the teachers conduct themselves with professionalism, utilize best practices in instruction, and keep their hands clean. But what happens when it all goes awry? How do we respond to substandard performance?

Three Layers of Discontent

Inadequate performance in teaching is not always easy to define. Sure, sometimes a teacher arrives on campus drunk, drives his Cadillac El Dorado through the hallways blaring Guns N' Roses, and destroys the statue of the school mascot, but that is a special case. Most teaching indiscretions are subtle. The trick for administrators is to identify the issue, then to grasp it head-on in the most appropriate manner. Let's have a look at the three layers of performance concerns:

Caught with hands in the cookie jar. This one is easy: The teacher violates a law, disregards policy repeatedly, or is observed doing something so stupid that it's hard to imagine anyone would do it. That is, until we read the newspaper and see that this isn't the first time someone's been this stupid, either. These folks need personnel discipline, and the course is clear-cut. Call H. R.

A slip of the lip. We're all entitled to a mess-up. Golfers call them "mulligans." These are uncharacteristically bad moves: a frustrated teacher uses sarcasm in the classroom; a tired teacher omits an entire morning in her lesson plans; a harried teacher inadvertently checks out 25 copies of the wrong book and decides to just show a video instead while she pulls herself together; a confused teacher forgets it's Monday and spends the day at Sea World instead of in his sixth grade classroom. Unless this becomes a weekly habit, all these folks need is a wake-up call and a little nudge back in the right direction.

The silent assassin. More likely than the isolated incidents that are listed above, however, are the common, repeated abrasions of Teacher Y outlined below. And, sadly, these situations repeat themselves far too often.

See if this sounds familiar: Teacher Y (as in, *"why* does he still come to work?") arrives at school just a few seconds after the contracted start-time, but before the kids arrive. He fills the daily routine with unimaginative lessons, or perhaps gives scripted instruction with no ties to any specific learning outcomes; he has dispassionate relationships with his students. There may even be times the teacher simply sits at his desk while the students work. Teacher Y sits with his colleagues at lunchtime, but only to complain a bit and to shovel some leftovers hurriedly. When he's invited to stay after school to discuss the results of the math assessment, he declines (again) and hurries off with a stack of papers to mark—with no helpful feedback, mind you.

The teachers complain about his lack of collaboration. The parents complain about his lack of communication. The students complain about his lack of personality. He complains about whatever the topic *du jour* may be. And the student achievement in his class is just okay. Nothing special, but nothing out of a Quentin Tarantino movie, either. You're the principal. What do you do?

The Ugly Reality

We don't do much. We sit and close our eyes to it, with a grimace, yes, but still feeble and hapless. Technically, there's nothing Teacher Y is doing that qualifies as neglect of duty, that violates the teaching contract, or that would earn him a trip in the back of the sheriff's cruiser, cuffed and stuffed.

Morally, ethically, and realistically, though, Teacher Y is committing educational malpractice. We need to admit it: We have tons of research to support the "best practices" of instruction that he's ignoring; we have decades of qualitative and quantitative data to defend the cultivation of a nurturing classroom environment that he's disregarding; and we have reams of evidence to endorse the cultivation of true collaborative professional relationships that he's snubbing.

When will we take a stand against this malpractice? I say that time is now. *Right now*. If there are children in that classroom, or if there are going to be children in that classroom tomorrow, we have an obligation to provide the best possible learning environment—and to insist upon excellence from those in the noblest of professions.

What Do We Do?

Like I wrote several hundred words ago, our responsibility as principals is to inspire, motivate, and maximize the impact of our teachers on student learning. We can't wait until the teacher's performance evaluation is due and then submit a blind-sided scorcher. That wouldn't be right and it wouldn't help.

Instead, do this: Get courageous. Invite the teacher into your office to chat. Right now. Immediately, as in, *"What are you waiting for?"*

When that conversation begins, find out what's going on. Share your concerns. Talk about the specifics of what you've observed in that classroom. Get Teacher Y to talk about what's going on. Discuss. Argue. Exchange ideas. Converse. Reason. Get a real row going. Only when it's out in the open can we even begin to put a dent in its shell of artificial harmony and the "culture of nice."

Then, and only then, we can tackle a solution together. Share your expectations very, very clearly. Lay out the specifics. Create a plan. Write it down, commit to it, and include dates for observations and reviews. Enlist Teacher Y's suggestions and ideas. Isolate an approach that will inspire, motivate, and maximize the impact of this teacher on student learning. This is the noblest of professions we're talking about—it's worth that discomfort, that effort, and that openness. We can't shy away from our consciences.

The Bull's-Eye of School Discipline

Remember that time when there was a line of students awaiting their punishments outside your office door? Misbehaviors were running rampant, like ants on a picnic lunch. The school day was a blur of black eyes, name-calling, and disobedience. And it seemed like you spent your whole day disciplining young people for their naughty ways and misdeeds. That was this morning, really? Oh, you mean that happens every day?

Don't Cry "Foul" Quite Yet!

You, fellow administrator, are not alone. If you've been able to get out of your office long enough to visit a neighboring school, you've noticed there's a whole lot of malfeasance cramming school hallways. Every generation of educators has faced this debacle with a similar view, attributing the shenanigans of youth to a lack of respect for authority, poor upbringing, materialism, ignorance about the importance of education, or rock and roll music.

Whatever the reason, "kids today" just aren't as well-behaved as the kids were yesterday. Or that's what we've told ourselves. And we've said it enough times, with enough conviction, that we believe it. We could run for office on that platform!

When it comes to schoolwide discipline and management, the questions shouldn't be, "What are the parents feeding those kids in the morning?" Rather (and not just because usually *we* are the ones feeding the kids in the morning), the question is, "What are we doing about it?" Are we:

A. admiring the problem from all angles, like a Cellini sculpture
B. reacting by "doing" discipline and getting angry
C. ignoring it and hoping it goes away, like "Wife Swap"
D. taking a proactive approach to reclaiming our schools

If we wisely chose option D, then we're well on our way. For the rest of us, we need to forget Renaissance art and reality TV for a second so we can redouble our efforts to help students acclimate to life at school. Tap into each of these children and make a connection strong enough that each one will want to play by the rules, and make school a place worth showing up to every morning. In order to do that, we're going to have to pull ourselves up by our bootstraps, focus on the center of the bull's-eye, and get on with it.

The Almighty Locus of Control

We need tighter discipline, correct? Sure, but it turns out it's not discipline, per se, that we need. It's *relationships*. In particular, it's the relationships that students have with others, both adults and children, that have a more direct effect on their behaviors, attitudes, and general well-being than any other single factor in the school environment.

Let's view our bull's-eye from the outside-in:

Whole-school factors. As much as we'd like to believe it, the structures and protocol we have in place schoolwide (the way kids line up, the awards we hand out at assemblies, the penalties we assign) are not the answer to creating suddenly rule-abiding masses. Rules and systemwide consequences are fine and dandy, and they lend a certain semblance of order to the grounds, but they're only the tip of the iceberg. (Sorry for mixing metaphors, it's an occupational hazard.)

Grade-level (or subject-area, or team) factors. In today's educational landscape, where teacher collaboration is the norm, many adults have the opportunity to get to know each child quite well. (Here we begin hitting on the theme of *relationships* again.) This structure provides several adults with leverage to work with students on appropriate behaviors, motivation, and developing such novel concepts as "work ethic" and "responsibility."

Classroom culture factors. Where do students spend most of their time at school? No, not in the restrooms smoking cigarettes—that was a different generation, back before all of today's unruliness hit. In the classroom, that's where you'll find them! If classrooms are established as places of mutual respect, places of investigation and learning, places of positive energy, and places of predictable order, it follows that the children occupying them will likewise demonstrate proper conduct. This is because they'll be busy working and getting educated together.

Student-peer factors. There comes a time in every child's life when fellow children become interesting. That time is called "childhood," and it lasts well into the late teens. (Even longer for human males, or so my wife tells me.) For verification, what do most children do when they have a bit of free time? No, they don't tease the girls and run—that was eons ago. Yes, they seek out other children to play with, hang with, run with, and cavort with. Most children search for other similar children—by interests, looks, abilities, behaviors, senses of humor, attitudes, fashion sense, or other characteristics. So how are we helping to encourage and shape friendships, alliances, and playmates? This falls under the scope of our jurisdiction at school, and its value ought not to be underestimated.

Student-teacher factors. Bull's-eye. Think back to your own school days. Sure, there was some rock-throwing at windows, but ignore that for a moment. What kept the raft together (another mixed metaphor, sorry) was the gentle, nurturing, kind hand of the teacher. If that didn't work, it was the tough, assertive, demanding hand of the teacher. When all else failed, it was the direct, familiar, respected hand of the teacher. This is as close to the "problem" as we can get. Research, experience, and common sense combine to tell us that each individual student's relationship with his or her teacher is the most directly correlated school factor that influences behavior.

Relationships, relationships, relationships. We know they matter. The key is to cultivate them, to grow respectful, responsible, resilient children—from the bull's-eye out.

You, fine reader, have probably noticed that there is no "Family" circle in our target. This omission was intentional for two reasons: One, for some of our most troubled students who have the most difficulty acquiescing to school expectations, the family is not always a source of consistent support. Two, the student's family is not necessarily under our control, though it is in the sphere of our influence, and this target emphasizes where we ought to focus our energy to yield the greatest benefit.

Before "Lightning" Strikes

Let's start this discussion with a quiz. Please answer honestly, and pay attention—the questions are tricky. Answer *yes* or *no*.

- ♦ Have you ever disciplined a student at school?
- ♦ Have you ever disciplined the same student more than once?
- ♦ Do you feel like you spend the majority of your discipline-time handling the same group of students over and over again?
- ♦ Do you have these students' parents' phone numbers on speed-dial on your cell phone?
- ♦ Does the sight of these students in the hallways induce some sort of an involuntary physical response in you, perhaps gastrointestinal?

◆ Have you had serious chats with your spouse, children, neighbors, neighbors' children, and other far-away acquaintances and asked them to *not* name their unborn children the same names as these students?

If you answered "Yes" to any (or, more likely, *all)* of the questions above, congratulations! You're officially a principal.

If you answered "No" to any (or all) of the questions above, there's only one question left: How's the weather there in Lake Wobegon?

A widely acknowledged reality in education is that children, on occasion, misbehave. This is no big deal, as we have structures set up in schools to handle misbehaviors and the students responsible for them. Most schools have a set of consequences, a formal behavior gradient, and/or a progressive discipline plan. And to administer the lion's share of this discipline, most schools have a principal.

Discipline is a funny idea. When we take a good look at the data, in most of our schools we find that a striking minority wreak the majority of the havoc. So we principals spend an inordinate amount of time on the phone with a few students' parents, chasing the same runners down the hallway, supervising them in the office, holding them back from a tantrum, blocking them from leaving the building, ushering them away from conflicts, and counseling them against their bad choices.

It's an exhausting cycle: students cause mischief, we react to misbehaviors, we punish the students, we restore order and wait for the students to cause more and greater mischief. Around and around we go with the Frequent Fliers, the Repeat Offenders, the Office Boomerangs, the Detention Crew. These are the students that have difficulty, for one reason or another, playing by the rules, following directions, and keeping themselves out of trouble.

These students make up the Lightning Club. Because lightning can strike at any time, virtually without warning. But why wait for the lightning to strike? Why not act in a proactive manner? Benjamin Franklin didn't invent the lightning rod in 1752 for fun. He did it to help dissipate safely underground the electrical charge from lightning, thereby sparing tall buildings and other structures from certain damage. It was a proactive approach.

The Lighting Club in Action

The Lightning Club, as outlined by my good friend and colleague Derek Cordell in his article, "A Vaccine for School Discipline," is a proactive model of schoolwide behavior management and discipline. It's about building relationships, empowering students, and strengthening positive behavioral habits.

The Lightning Club consists of four real-life steps:

Identify the students that have the highest need for support. You might think this is the easiest step, since the children in question might be lined up outside your office door right now. Teachers and counselors might have some good input, so a key to this step is to be collaborative. Not every student that throws a pencil in class, shoves a classmate in line, or fills the urinal with Tic Tacs warrants membership because the model can become unwieldy if the list grows too long. Keep it to the highest-need, highest-risk, highest-frequency lightning bolts.

Create a plan of success for each individual student. In collaboration with the teachers, counselor, parents, *and student,* sit down and isolate the top behavior (or two) that is most negatively impacting the student's (and his or her classmates') educational experience. Write the detailed expectations of behavior, short-term and long-term goals, and include a series of small, sequential rewards for the student to earn for realizing success *together.* This success plan is the backbone of a productive collaborative relationship between all the stakeholders in the equation.

Make frequent, intentional positive contact with each individual student. According to the Search Institute, there are 40 developmental assets critical to the growth and success of healthy adolescents. Included in this list: support from three or more non-parent adults. These children, even more than any others, truly need to bond with key adults. So talk to them, ask how their weekends went, give them high-fives in the hallway, smile across the lunchroom at them, make a special point to ask about their schoolwork while you are conducting classroom walk-throughs, shoot hoops on the playground with them—whatever contact you can make, make it. Then call their parents and tell them how much you enjoy seeing their child smile at school. When we build those strong relationships, the positive behaviors will follow.

Follow through with the success plan faithfully, consistently, and devotedly. If you need the push, ask the school counselor, another teacher, head custodian, or paraprofessional to log positive contacts with you (in a friendly, child-focused competition). Set goals for yourself to make three positive contacts with each Lightning Club member every day. Set aside time to debrief each week's results with the teacher and the child (and the parent, if possible)—this can be as simple as a short "How'd the week go?" form and a quick phone call home. Of course, it is also essential to provide the small rewards on schedule. Celebrate successes and reinvigorate the stakeholders as often as possible—again, success begets success: positive behaviors will follow.

It's easy for principals, teachers, counselors, custodians, and crossing guards to dread the presence of the rabble-rousers. It's simple to think, "What swear-words and disrespectful behavior is she going to share today?" or, "It's just a matter of time before he flips out and gets into another fight." It's uncomfortable to face them, again and again, and it's natural to want to avoid the strain and anguish of constantly disciplining them. No one likes being struck by lightning. But remember, Harry Wong fans, these are mis*behaviors*, not mis*children.*

And is it really so difficult to install a conductive-metal strip with a low-resistance wire buried in the ground (with slight adaptations for behavior modification purposes in the schoolhouse, of course)?

Charismatic Leaders and Ego

Think, for a moment, of the five or six greatest leaders you've ever heard of, known, worked for, or imagined . . .

As you consider those leaders past and present, what are the characteristics that define them? What makes them great? Are they effective because of situational work, interpersonal dealings, general intelligence, content expertise, or perhaps a little of each? Do they possess that "je ne sais quoi" that we hear so much about but really don't know how to spell? Write down a couple of words, thoughts, or descriptions that match these impactful individuals.

As you engaged in that quick exercise, your mind probably raced with thoughts of wonderful leaders from your own life (maybe a favorite teacher or coach), mixed with some great historical leaders (like John F. Kennedy or Martin Luther King, Jr.), and sprinkled with a few outstanding leaders about whom you have heard but know very little. That last group probably consisted of rather charismatic personalities—Chrysler chairman Lee Iacocca or former Boston Celtics basketball coach Red Auerbach, for example.

Some might caution us against blindly following charismatic leaders, meaning those who can woo the room, whip the crowd into frenzy, and entice an emotional reaction out of any situation. Michael Fullan, for instance, warns us that "Charismatic leaders inadvertently often do more harm than good because, at best, they provide episodic improvement followed by frustrated or despondent dependency," and, worse still, "they are role models who can never be emulated."

I respectfully add a caveat by cautioning against the blind following of *any* leader, charismatic or otherwise. And, in defense of all our charismatic colleagues out there leading schools and realizing tremendous success, charisma is *not* a personality deficit.

Sometimes a powerful, suave, or engaging personality is exactly what the situation dictates. When leading soldiers into a dangerous battle, a field marshal must rouse the troops to follow. When entering an important fiscal period, a brokerage manager must inspire the agents to increase their productivity. And when facing increased public accountability and higher standards, school superintendents must rally their masses to refocus on the mission and vision of student achievement. Principals, in their school buildings, are no different.

Charisma is a positive human characteristic. A leader who possesses it has an extraordinary ability to connect with his or her followers, link them to the goal, and motivate them to pursue the common vision. If a charismatic leader can use that interpersonal skill while remaining focused on the correct path, even as it changes underfoot, he or she will have the most vital commodity in leadership: followers. Or, more aptly stated in the educational scheme: partners on the journey.

Ego and the Principalship

Just as charisma can play an important role in leadership, so can ego. Leaders must not only want to be in the position of responsibility, they must believe that their impact is required in order to achieve success. In *The One Thing You Need to Know*, Marcus Buckingham states, "From all my interviews with effective leaders I cannot think of one example in which the person lacked this craving to be at the helm, charting the course ahead."

That strong ego cannot go unbridled, of course. Effective leaders find a way to channel their egos into a productive outlet for the organization. Ordinarily, the individuals we're talking about here are not the egomaniacal "It's all about me!" type of leaders. Rather, we're talking about folks who seek out challenges, who laugh in the face of danger, and who revel in the opportunity to stand at the bow and lead us into battle.

Jim Collins explains that the truly exceptional leaders, his Level 5 leaders, "are incredibly ambitious—but their ambition is first and foremost for the institution, not themselves." The problems arise when the leaders confuse themselves with the vision and put their own desires ahead of their organizations. We have seen this in recent history in the cases of Enron's high-profile corporate greed and Martha Stewart's insider training conviction. In less public settings, we've heard about leaders who got "too big for their britches." We've all probably known or worked for an employer who let his own needs outweigh the good of the whole. The real danger occurs, however, when followers become so enthralled with a leader that they follow without thinking critically about the leader's vision.

Cultivating Charisma

What does this mean for us as educational leaders? Simply put, since we acknowledge that leaders who are charismatic and self-confident (the politically-correct term for possessing a strong ego) are likely to be effective in their leadership, then we ought to cultivate those traits. Or, at the very least, not try to hide them.

- ♦ We can learn to woo, even if it isn't our innate strength. We can practice and practice, because eventually we're going to need to "win others over" to garner support for initiatives, programs, or fund-raisers.
- ♦ We can project an air of confidence, for our conviction is echoed in the teaching staffs that depend on us. They need to trust that their leader believes in the mission, the direction, and the battle.
- ♦ We ought not to shy away from our naturally strong ego and urge to stand in the front of the crowd. Someone's going to have to ride that horse back and forth in front of the rank and file, urging them onward, inspiring them with timeless words and emotional motivation. It may as well be the leader.
- ♦ We shouldn't pretend that charming others is a sin. This is a strategy humans have used for millennia— getting people on our side helps us accomplish difficult tasks.

None of that is wrong if, above all else, we remain steadfastly true to our mission. With an eye on the prize and structures in place to ensure that the path is valid, a charismatic leader could well garner the proper support and inspiration to move people quickly, efficiently, and encouragingly forward. Let's tap into that list of great-leader characteristics and lead the charge.

Panning for Gold in the Era of Accountability

I'm a practitioner in the public schools. I hold the enviable post of school principal. I've now been in the school system long enough to see that the pendulum does indeed swing back and forth between one irrational extreme to the other. We've had nationwide school improvement initiatives since Sputnik, A Nation at Risk, Welcome Back Kotter, the No Child Left

Behind Act, and Race to the Top. Each one refocused our attention on what we deem most essential: student learning and the effectiveness of our current school system. This is good.

You may have also noticed that, over the past several years, thousands of American schools have awoken to find themselves fallen out of the bed of favor with the American public, landing sharply on the floor of tacks attached to NCLB consequences. This is not so good.

Does a spot on the "in need of improvement" list define a school? Are the cumulative experiences of the children within a school's walls rendered moot after the test scores arrive? Is every school on the "list" offering a sub-par education to the children on its roster? Is AYP (Adequate Yearly Progress) the sole determining factor of effectiveness?

I understand the realities of the push for proficiency, the harsh consequences tied to education today, and the public perception accompanying school designations. I also understand that perception is reality, and many schools absorb an undeserved beating in the public eye because of a blurry snapshot of student performance.

So in order to shift the perception, and concurrently the reality, we need to provide a pretty image for the public to view. Nobody is going to do this for us; we need to grab the cameras ourselves, shoot a series of images, and share the shots that matter. I suggest the following prints for your schoolhouse darkroom:

Know your data. Test scores are nice, but dig beyond the obvious AYP profile. Scour grades, longitudinal growth charts, individual student reports, formative assessments, and any numerical representation hidden in the information tonnage we keep regarding student achievement. Pearls are usually hidden in oysters, I believe. Find them.

Know your program. Know it like your favorite hat knows the contours of your head. Speak intelligently about the changes your school has made, why they were important and well-timed innovations, what your expectations are for future success, and give ridiculously specific details about current progress. When you are at a barbeque, your neighbor's obnoxious buddy will ask you, "What's so great about your school?" Be prepared to fly your banner right then and there.

Know your students. Which students are progressing rapidly, and which are flailing? Which are proficient, which are not, and which are tantalizingly close to making the grade? Which children are happy, well-adjusted, critical thinkers capable of considerably influencing their surrounding mates? Which are the silent, still, invisible children? What are their names? What drives them to succeed, to work, to strive? When you take a look at what's really important, you'll see in their eyes the reflections of our true mission. You can share that.

Know the highlights. Keep a file in your office cabinet labeled, "Stuff to write home about." Children say funny things, and they're always entertaining to record for recitals at the Cask 'n Flagon on some Friday night. But what I'm suggesting here is recording the good moments that instill pride in all involved. Did your school receive a grant, have a bookmark-contest winner, obtain local recognition, score well on a facilities inspection report, receive a donation of books, or improve even two percent on a grade-level spelling inventory? Keep the highlights fresh in your mind, and be prepared to share them. Folks love hearing the feel-good stories, and we simply don't share them enough.

Be proactive. Share the highlights, data, and positive tales at carefully crafted intervals. Coax, cajole, or guilt the correct people into the audience when you take the stage. Here are some introductory suggestions for the sharing modes:

◆ Create a school brochure. What better way to concisely provide all the information you deem necessary in a handy format? Send it to the School Board, all residents of your school's neighborhood, your mother-in-law's pool guy, or anyone who might like to raise their brows at a professional educational institution.

◆ Host a carnival on the school grounds. An Open House would work, also, with games and fun activities for the whole family. Spread some positive thoughts about the school itself, even if academics aren't even on the menu. Welcome all comers, without attempting to fundraise, and thank everyone for visiting the greatest school in the United States.

◆ Invite local politicians. Invite board members, press reporters, local car dealers, and anyone else who might benefit from seeing the excellence within your school's walls firsthand. For a targeted invitation, prepare a short reader's theater, student performance, or a specific component of your schoolwide program to center your focus. Then get the guests out of there, with a "wow" on their lips.

◆ Fancy up the entryway. Nothing welcomes a family more openly into a school than an embracing foyer. I once worked in a school that wanted to protect its flowers, so the custodians strung up "caution" tape around the bed. That sent the families a strong message, didn't it? We spent a Saturday building a split-rail fence to replace the yellow tape, then we had an artist paint a cheerful mural just inside the front door. Easy. Inviting. Open.

The key is simple: We want to preempt the negative views and comments about our schools. Before folks ask, "What's wrong with your school?" we shall offer the dissenting opinion, packaged handsomely in a series of 8 × 10 glossies, matted and framed for distribution.

Sure, it might be easier to lament the "unfunded mandate," bemoan the stress on testing rather than educating, and long for the days of yore before the assault of acronyms, but what would that solve? Our voices would be lost in the cacophony. Why not strip away the veneer and expose the silver lining that enshrouds even the darkest clouds? You've got the canvas just sitting there, waiting. Paint your picture.

REFLECTION QUESTIONS

In Part IV, you considered strategies specific to the role of the building principal. How do these challenge your thinking about the impact and duties of the principalship? Use the following questions to guide your thinking about the ideas presented in Part IV and the strategies you'll employ to implement them to motivate yourself or others. Then make it happen.

1. List the first five words that come to your mind when describing the job of a school principal. Did you record the words "balanced," "control," "peaceful," "perspective," or their synonyms? Why or why not? What would it take for you to be able to use those descriptors accurately one year from now?

2. Stephen Covey's Time Management Matrix can be a supremely helpful tool for prioritization. Jot down the top 50 tasks you perform as a principal (or whatever job you currently hold), then plot them on a TMM. Where do you spend the majority of your time and energy? If you reflect upon your mission, where *should* you focus your attention? How can you realign that focus? Then, how can you motivate others to realign their focus also?

3. How can you tell if your staff is truly collaborating? What are the tell-tale signs? What specific actions have you taken to build that collaborative environment? What are your next steps? How can you motivate your staff to engage in the learning process necessary for growth?

4. Reread "Mentoring and the Three Golden Rules" and list the three golden rules on a note card of some sort. Next to each, write down two steps you take to follow that rule on a regular basis. Then, next to that, craft a question that you can use to prompt yourself to remember the rule and to keep your focus on point. Put that note card someplace handy as a self-motivation tool.

5. What is the single most important factor affecting student achievement? What is your single greatest asset as a building leader? The answers are the same: quality teachers. Every job opening you post should be treated with reverence. Can you exclaim, emphatically, that every position

you've filled lately has met the required "Six steps to hiring" outlined in "Teacher Selection Counts"? If not, how can you pledge to ensure only the highest-quality hires from now on?

6. How do you use the teacher evaluation process to build teachers' capacity instead of a hoop that your staff must jump through every spring? Can you create, implement, and follow an annual timeline that includes capacity-building activities throughout the year for each of the teachers under your watch? Try it—even with just a few teachers this year—and record how it changes the climate of those professional conversations and the evaluation process. Do any of the teachers demonstrate increased motivation? How so?

7. Most school discipline is enacted as a reaction to a student's misbehaviors. What structures do you currently have in place to work proactively with the student body? Talk to five colleagues, ask them the same question, and record their responses. Now you'll have a bank of strategies you can implement. How might they fit into your school's climate and culture?

8. Describe yourself in three to five words. Go ahead, brag a bit. Write them down. Whatever you wrote, as long as it's honest, is perfectly fine. Do you enjoy leadership? Why or why not? What about leading others is fun? What do you look forward to? What gets your adrenaline flowing? How can you arrange your schedule and priorities to ensure you engage in those activities more often?

9. Why might people want to follow you? What characteristics do you possess that match the definition of "leader"? Is it your words? Your vision? Your actions? Contemplate this for a while, then consider this: What am I willing to learn that will enable me to motivate those who I haven't been able to reach yet?

Conclusion

First of all, please allow me to thank you for reading this anthology of essays. It is doubtful that each entry met unilateral adulation and spurred an onslaught of action for each of you. However, it is my desire to generate thought, for thought propels action, and action leads to change, and change leads to growth, and growth leads to excellence.

Each essay was written at a particular time, for a particular purpose, because of a particular incident. As a school principal, I have the good fortune to work with literally hundreds of people in thousands of interactions on a daily basis—quite a field of opportunities to draw from, I'd say.

The majority of these interactions require me to engage in motivation of some form or another. Overwhelmingly, I'm moved to inspire others to take action, to consider alternatives, to reflect upon possibilities, to encourage risk-taking, to instigate movement, to arouse emotion, to compel confidence, or to assert courage. That's what leadership is all about.

My expectation, then, is that these essays, and the ideas contained therein, will serve to generate thought in you, as leaders yourselves, as well as provide an avenue for you to generate that thought in the people you lead. I can tell you, quite honestly, that I've used them over the years to get myself up and out of bed in the morning just as much as I've used them to rally the troops around an idea whose time has come.

And just in case you need just one more compelling stimulus to spur you onward and upward, here's a bonus essay to help you keep your priorities focused, your weapons sharpened, your wheels greased, and your determination fierce. Go get 'em!

There Is No Tomorrow

Let's go back to Quadrant II, folks. This is where I'm going to plant you, water you, and provide you with sunshine, nourishment, and TLC. Quadrant II, as you'll recall, is where Stephen Covey's Time Management Matrix (from *The 7 Habits of Highly Effective People*) shows the behaviors that are characterized by High Importance but Low Urgency. That means, Quadrant II actions are those that will lead to success and growth, so you must definitely, assuredly, and unquestionably do them, but you don't necessarily need to start right now. We can handle them later.

If not now, when? If not me, who? If I can't pass GO, when do I collect $200?

In *Rocky III*, boxing-rival-turned-supporter Apollo Creed embarked upon a quest to train our hero, Rocky Balboa, as he prepared to fight the menacing powerhouse Clubber Lane. Rocky didn't have his game-face on during a sparring session, and Apollo screamed, "This guy will kill you! What's the matter with you?" An exhausted, clearly unfocused Rocky told Apollo, "Tomorrow. I'll do it tomorrow."

Apollo bellowed an emphatic, reverberating response: "There is no tomorrow!"

When I was a middle-school Spanish teacher, I had set the lofty goal to have a 1:1 conversation with each of the 150 students under my charge. I knew about the power of relationships, and I figured it was important for me to get to know the big kids in my classes as people. This was at least as important as it was for me to figure out if they knew how to conjugate both forms of the verb "to be," or if they understood the difference between masculine and feminine nouns and how that affects the adjectives describing them.

Make no mistake, the students in my six classes were amazing. I had the privilege to teach children who were bound and determined to be doctors, lawyers, college athletes, teachers, scientists, international business translators, diplomats, and to accomplish all sorts of wondrous deeds. Those who didn't have concrete plans still inspired me with their hopes and dreams for family, world peace, and launching Internet startups in Egypt; they regaled me with tales of community service, an abundance of activities, and incredible talents.

In fact, it was during this year as a middle-school teacher that my thoughts about the future were the brightest. If these were the future adults in charge of running our nation, we were in good hands.

I didn't get to all the students, however. There were a few whose schedules were so busy, or they were so consumed with other activities, that I wasn't able to corner them for a chat. One student in my fourth-period class, who selected the Spanish codename "Pavo" because it means "turkey" and he was a bit of a class clown, was particularly evasive when I asked him to talk. I even tried to get him to spend a minute or two during class work-time, but he'd say, "Señor Pete, I have to finish this."

"No problema," I replied, "Vamos a hablar mañana."

When he looked quizzically at me, I'd say, "That means we'll talk tomorrow." He'd nod. This pattern repeated itself for a couple of weeks into the school year.

When the news came one morning that our friend Pavo had chosen to end his own life with a shotgun, I faced undoubtedly the most challenging event of my career. Two statements hit me square on the forehead: 1) I have to address his class today, and 2) there is no mañana.

At no point did the message sink in more than at the beginning of fourth period that day, when we all stared silently, through teary eyes, at Pavo's empty chair in the front-center of the horseshoe-shaped arrangement. If I hadn't already known, deep down, that *right now* is the time to take action, I learned it then.

Right Now, Indeed

If we were to pit two great historical figures in opposite corners in the ring to duke it out, who would win a sparring match between these two: Thomas Jefferson and Mark Twain? Sure, Twain authored such illustrious titles as "Concerning

Chambermaids" and "The Story of the Bad Little Boy Who Didn't Come to Grief," but I think I'll have to give the nod to the first U.S. Secretary of State. Why? Consider their quotes about procrastination:

Jefferson: "Never put off 'til tomorrow what you can do today."

Twain: "Never put off 'til tomorrow what you can do the day after tomorrow."

Jefferson wins by knockout.

It doesn't matter what field of work we're in. Educators, contractors, stock brokers, city planners, truck drivers, boxers, and gold prospectors (one of Twain's first dismal attempts at making a living, by the way) all have steps they need to take to become successful. Greater levels of effectiveness await, excellence is within reach of all of us—usually through some combination of training, goal-setting, professional development, education, skill acquisition, continued learning, and perseverance.

In other words, the fruit on the tippity-top branches dangle imminently for us, if we're willing to put forth the effort to pick it. Effort, that's the key. Hard work. Energy. Determination. Focus. Dedication. Initiative. Gusto. Hustle.

Sure, we could plod along, generically happy with the status quo, in the ruts and routines of our daily work. We all have "to-do" lists. We all have deadlines. We all receive orders. We all have a host of colleagues, supervisors, and constituents pestering us for answers, for results, for action, for *stuff*. If it would make us happy, we could meander blandly through our lives, claiming the hectic nature of our work, the increasing pace of our lives, and the relentless demands of our time leave us precious little opportunity to make the moves that will lead us to personal and professional enlightenment. And plenty of people do that—we know who they are. They're the people in our lives who consistently talk about how things are happening to them and how their lives are out of control. Sometimes they use the words, "If only," as if someone else were in charge of their decisions.

For the rest of us, the event-makers, we'll swap "if only" for "right now:"

RIGHT NOW I could start working on my advanced degree.

RIGHT NOW I could stop being so consumed by reading e-mails and memos.

RIGHT NOW I could move my "to-do" list off the top of my "to-do" list.

RIGHT NOW I could focus my attention on the behaviors that'll move me forward.

RIGHT NOW I could talk to the people who will help me.

RIGHT NOW I could always strive to be a better me.

What are the goals you'd like to accomplish? What gains would you like to make? What are the actions you need to take? What are you waiting for? Do it now, folks. There is no tomorrow.

References

Adams, J. T. (1931). *The epic of America.* New York, NY: Little, Brown, and Company.

Allington, R. L., & Cunningham, P. M. (2007). *Schools that work: Where all children read and write.* Boston, MA: Allyn and Bacon.

Blanchard, K. H. (1989). *The one minute manager meets the monkey.* New York, NY: William Morrow and Company, Inc.

Boudett, K. P. (2008). *Data wise: A step-by-step guide to using assessment results to improve teaching and learning.* Cambridge, MA: Harvard Education Press.

Buckingham, M. (2005). *The one thing you need to know . . . about great managing, great leading, and sustained individual success.* New York, NY: Free Press.

Buckingham, M., & Clifton, D. O. (2001). *Now, discover your strengths.* New York, NY: Free Press.

Buckingham, M., & Coffman, C. (1999). *First, break all the rules: What the world's greatest managers do differently.* New York, NY: Simon & Schuster.

Bussey, J. (2008, November 24). Failing our children. *Wall Street Journal.*

Collins, J. (2001). *Good to great: Why some companies make the leap . . . and others don't.* New York, NY: Harper Collins Publishers, Inc.

Cordell, D. (2008). The lightning club: A vaccine for school discipline. *The Launching Pad* 2(1). Retrieved from http://www .educationhall.com/TheLaunchingPad/WS08Lightning.htm

Covey, S. R. (1989). *The 7 habits of highly effective people.* New York, NY: Simon & Schuster.

Cox, L. (2006). *Grayson.* New York, NY: Random House.

Curwin, R. L., Mendler, A. N., & Mendler, B. D. (2008). *Discipline with dignity: New challenges, new solutions.* Alexandria, VA: Association for Supervision and Curriculum Development.

Danielson, C. (2007). *Enhancing professional practice: A framework for teaching.* Alexandria, VA: Association for Supervision and Curriculum Development.

Danielson, C. (2006). *Teacher leadership that strengthens professional practice.* Alexandria, VA: Association for Supervision and Curriculum Development.

Dewey, J. (1910). *How we think.* Boston, MA: Heath and Company.

Dr. Seuss. (1989). *And to think that I saw it on mulberry street*. New York, NY: Random House.

Dufour, R. (1998). *Professional learning communities at work: Best practices for enhancing student achievement*. Bloomington, IN: National Education Service.

Earl, L. M., & Katz, S. (2006). *Leading schools in a data-rich world: Harnessing data for school improvement*. Thousand Oaks, CA: Corwin Press.

Edmonds, R. (1979). Effective schools for the urban poor. *Educational Leadership 37*(1), 15–24.

EducationWorld. (2011). Administrator's Desk. Retrieved from http://www.educationworld.com/a_admin/

Fleming, I. (1954). *Live and let die*. New York, NY: Jove Publications.

Fullan, M. (2007). *Leading in a culture of change*. San Francisco, CA: Jossey-Bass.

Fullan, M. (2003). *Change forces with a vengeance*. New York, NY: Routledge Falmer.

Green, A. C., & Webster, J. C. (1994). *Victory: The principles of championship living*. Lake Mary, FL: Creation House.

Guskey, T. (2002). Does it make a difference? Evaluating professional development. *Educational Leadership 59*(6), 45–51.

Hall, P. (2009). On leadership in schools. *The Launching Pad 3*(1). Retrieved from http://educationhall.com/TheLaunchingPad/WS09Leadership.htm

Hall, P. (2009). An open letter to a new principal. *Principal 88*(4), 9–13.

Hall, P., & Simeral, A. (2008). *Building teachers' capacity for success: A collaborative approach for coaches and school leaders*. Alexandria, VA: Association for Supervision and Curriculum Development.

Hall, P. (2008). Building bridges: Strengthening the principal induction process through intentional mentoring. *Phi Delta Kappan 89*(6), 449–452.

Hall, P. (2005). The principal's presence and supervision to improve teaching. *SEDL 17*(2), 12–16.

Hall, P. (2005). A school reclaims itself. *Educational Leadership 62*(5), 70–73.

Hall, P. A. (2004). *The first-year principal*. Lanham, MD: Scarecrow Press.

Hattie, J. (2008). *Visible learning: A synthesis of over 800 meta-analyses relating to achievement*. New York, NY: Routledge.

Heifetz, R. A. (1994). *Leadership without easy answers*. Cambridge, MA: Harvard University Press.

Dalai Lama & Cutler, H. C. (1998). *The art of happiness: A handbook for living*. New York, NY: Riverhead Books.

Hook, S. (1943). *The hero in history: A study in limitation and possibility.* New York, NY: The John Day Company.

Johnson, S. (2010). *The present: The gift for changing times.* New York, NY: Broadway Books.

Johnson, S., & Blanchard, K. (1998). *Who moved my cheese?: An amazing way to deal with change in your work and in your life.* New York, NY: Putnam.

Johnson, S., & Johnson, C. (1988). *The one minute teacher: How to teach others to teach themselves.* New York, NY: Harper Paperbacks.

Kennedy, J. F. (1961). *Special message to the congress on education.* Retrieved from http://www.jfklink.com/speeches/jfk/publicpapers/1961/jfk46_61.html

Locke, E. (1968). Toward a theory of task motivation and incentives. *Organizational Behavior and Human Performance 3*(2), 157–189.

Marshall, K. (2006). What's a principal to do? *Education Week 86*(1), 17.

Marzano, R. J. (2007). *The art and science of teaching: A comprehensive framework for effective instruction.* Alexandria, VA: Association for Supervision and Curriculum Development.

Marzano, R. J. (2003). *What works in schools: Translating research into action.* Alexandria, VA: Association for Supervision and Curriculum Development.

Marzano, R. J., Pickering, D. J., & Pollock, J. E. (2001). *Classroom instruction that works: Research-based strategies for increasing student achievement.* Alexandria, VA: Association for Supervision and Curriculum Development.

Maxwell, J. C. (2005). *Thinking for a change: 11 ways highly successful people approach life and work.* Nashville, TN: Thomas Nelson.

Maxwell, J. C. (2000). *Failing forward: Turning mistakes into stepping stones for success.* Nashville, TN: Thomas Nelson.

Mays, W. (1988). *Say hey: The autobiography of Willie Mays.* New York, NY: Simon & Schuster.

Monroe, L. (1997). *Leadership lessons from inside and outside the classroom.* New York, NY: Public Affairs.

National Association of Elementary School Principals. (2007). *Leading learning communities: Standards for what principals should know and be able to do.* Alexandria, VA: National Association of Elementary School Principals.

National Board of Professional Teaching Standards (2011). *The five core propositions.* Retrieved from http://www.nbpts.org/the_standards/the_five_core_propositio

Odden, A. & Wallace, M. (2003). Leveraging teacher pay. *Education Week 22*(43), 64.

Patterson, K., Grenny, J., Maxfield, D., & McMillan, R. (2008). *Influencer: The power to change anything.* New York, NY: McGraw-Hill.

Pausch, R., & Zaslow, J. (2008). *The last lecture.* New York, NY: Hyperion.

Payne, R. K. (2005). *A framework for understanding poverty.* Highlands, TX: aha! Process, Inc.

Pink, D. H. (2009). *Drive: The surprising truth about what motivates us.* New York, NY: Riverhead Books.

Reeves, D. B. (2009). *Leading change in your school: How to conquer myths, build commitment, and get results.* Alexandria, VA: Association for Supervision and Curriculum Development.

Reeves, D. B. (2008). *Reframing teacher leadership to improve your school.* Alexandria, VA: Association for Supervision and Curriculum Development.

Reeves, D. B. (2006). *The learning leader: How to focus school improvement for better results.* Alexandria, VA: Association for Supervision and Curriculum Development.

Ripley, A. (2008, December 8). Can she save our schools? *Time Magazine.*

Schmoker, M. J. (2011). *Focus: Elevating the essentials to radically improve student learning.* Alexandria, VA: Association for Supervision and Curriculum Development.

Schmoker, M. J. (2006). *Results now: How we can achieve unprecedented improvements in teaching and learning.* Alexandria, VA: Association for Supervision and Curriculum Development.

Whitaker, T. (2002). *Dealing with difficult teachers* (2nd ed.). Larchmont, NY: Eye On Education.

Wolk, R. A. (2011). *Wasting minds: Why our education system is failing and what we can do about it.* Alexandria, VA: Association for Supervision and Curriculum Development.

Wooden, J., & Jamison, S. (2005). *Wooden on leadership: How to create a winning organization.* New York, NY: McGraw-Hill.

Zaslow, J. (2007, July 5). Blame it on Mr. Rogers. *Wall Street Journal.*

NOTES

NOTES